METACONSCIOUS ENTREPRENEUR

How to Harness the
Unlimited Power of
Consciousness and Energy to
Grow a Wildly Successful Business
That Changes the World

STACY HARTMANN

BALBOA.PRESS
A DIVISION OF HAY HOUSE

Copyright © 2021 Stacy Hartmann.

All rights reserved. No part of this book may be used or reproduced by any means, graphic, electronic, or mechanical, including photocopying, recording, taping or by any information storage retrieval system without the written permission of the author except in the case of brief quotations embodied in critical articles and reviews.

Balboa Press books may be ordered through booksellers or by contacting:

Balboa Press
A Division of Hay House
1663 Liberty Drive
Bloomington, IN 47403
www.balboapress.com
844-682-1282

Because of the dynamic nature of the Internet, any web addresses or links contained in this book may have changed since publication and may no longer be valid. The views expressed in this work are solely those of the author and do not necessarily reflect the views of the publisher, and the publisher hereby disclaims any responsibility for them.

The author of this book does not dispense medical advice or prescribe the use of any technique as a form of treatment for physical, emotional, or medical problems without the advice of a physician, either directly or indirectly. The intent of the author is only to offer information of a general nature to help you in your quest for emotional and spiritual well-being. In the event you use any of the information in this book for yourself, which is your constitutional right, the author and the publisher assume no responsibility for your actions.

Any people depicted in stock imagery provided by Getty Images are models, and such images are being used for illustrative purposes only. Certain stock imagery © Getty Images.

Print information available on the last page.

ISBN: 978-1-9822-7684-3 (sc)
ISBN: 978-1-9822-7686-7 (hc)
ISBN: 978-1-9822-7685-0 (e)

Library of Congress Control Number: 2021922878

Balboa Press rev. date: 12/09/2021

For every person who feels deep in their soul they are here to do something big for the world and courageously take the path less traveled to bring it to fruition.

Contents

Acknowledgments ix
Prologue xi
Introduction xiii

PART I
The Truth about Consciousness and Energy

Chapter 1   The First Precept: Everything Is Energy 1
Chapter 2   The Second Precept: You Are Whole and
                Complete Now and Always 4
Chapter 3   The Third Precept: You Can Instantly
                Bring Your Desires into Your reality 8
Chapter 4   The Fourth Precept: You Can Be 100
                Percent Spiritual and 100 Percent Human
                at the Same Time 11
Chapter 5   The Fifth Precept: Effort is Limited.
                Energy is Limitless. 14
Chapter 6   The Sixth Precept: Time Is an Illusion.
                You Have the Power to Slow it Down or
                Speed it Up Past, Present, and Future. 17
Chapter 7   The Seventh Precept: Your Level of
                Consciousness Creates Your Reality 20
Chapter 8   Understanding the Seven Levels of
                Consciousness 24

PART II
The Truth about Conscious Success and Abundance

Chapter 9   The Awareness Code 47
Chapter 10   The Alignment Code 57
Chapter 11   The Awaken Code 66

PART III
The Truth about Accelerated Growth in a Conscious Business

Chapter 12 Conscious Business Rule 1:
   Start a Movement and Not a Following 81
Chapter 13 Conscious Business Rule 2: Don't Be
   Someone Else's Clone. Do Your Own Thing 83
Chapter 14 Conscious Business Rule 3: Slow Down to
   Speed Up 86
Chapter 15 Conscious Business Rule 4:
   The More Chaotic Things Feel in the
   Human Realm, the More Organized They
   Are in the Spiritual Realm 90
Chapter 16 Conscious Business Rule 5: Quitting Is
   Starting 93
Chapter 17 Conscious Business Rule 6:
   The Customer Is Not Always Right 96
Chapter 18 Conscious Business Rule 7: You Were
   Born to Create and Not Just Consume 99
Chapter 19 Creating Unstoppable Synergy, Growth,
   and Abundance for the Highest Good of All 103

Acknowledgments

With immense gratitude to …

Paul, Reid, and Tate, for your unconditional love and support and for constantly showing me what is truly most important: living this beautiful, simple life with you.

Amy Turner and Ashley Brabec Colvin, for your support, partnership, collaboration, and commitment to bringing this work out into the world.

Shantini Rajah for your brilliant talents and contributions that brought this book to life.

Bruce D. Schneider, Luke Iorio, Joan Ryan, and the entire iPEC family of leaders, trainers, students, and the incredible support behind the scenes, thank you for the life-changing and ongoing opportunities to grow, learn, and contribute to our mission of increasing the consciousness of the world one person at a time.

Clients, mentors, and friends and family who helped with the creation of this book. I deeply appreciate you. Thank you for your presence in my life:

Adam Jerry, Adam Urbanski, Amber Duffney, Amy Mollitor, Andres Valencia, Angela Smith, Angie Gerber, Anna Brunmayr, Antoinette Beauchamp, Ashley Elich, Ashley Fernandez, Becky Foster, Bonnie Bailey, Brooke Kover, Carrie Saks, Catherine Cunningham, Catharine Peters, Cathy Ferringo, Cheryl Dalton, Christina Lord, Christine Light, Cindy Ebert, Clarence Demers, Crista Gallagher, Dali Litinski, Dana Canneto, Denise Carlson, Elaine O'Keefe, Erica Horowitz, Hailey Starr, Jacki Amato, James Wallace, Jenna Tracy, Jennifer Alembik, Jennifer O'Grady, Jessica Ramsey, Jessie Carr, Jim Ross, Joanna Platt, Jonny Richard, Kate

Wright, Kathy Powell Spaulding, Katie Brandt, Katie Corvaglia, Kelley Tremalgia, Kemba Samuel, Kim Freese, Kris Prochaska. Krista Resnick, Laura Banks, Laura Honeycutt, Lauren Levin Pla, Laurie Jonas, Lawrence Lussier, Leanne McClain, Lisa Nelson, Lisa Plain, Louis Marrissette, Lynn Myrick, Maira Folia, Manuela Powell, Margaret Alabi, Martina Felderman, Maureen Nelson, Melissa Kohlsdorf, Melissa Stephens, Melissa West, Michael Sipe, Michele Walter, Missy McCracken, Monica Kenton, Natalie Biesel, Neha Govil, Ombretta Mancini, P'Abu Rasheed, Piper Watson, Rebecca Johnson, Rita Hausken, Ruth Benitez, Sarah Kenny, Shane Wachlin, Shelley Zerr, Simone Alleyne, Socary Rodriguez, Susie Dickey, Teresa Anderberg, Theresa Murphy, Tina Matejka, Wendy Burich, Wendy Irwin, and Yelena Mugin.

Prologue

The beautiful red-tailed hawk made his first appearance outside my kitchen window that morning. I'd never seen such a magnificent bird in the woods behind my house. He landed majestically on a tree stump, and he seemed to gaze right at me. I knew his arrival was an unmistakable sign from the God/Source/Universe—or GUS as I like to call this unimaginably vast and loving energy—and I intuitively understood what the hawk represented. It was like he was saying, "Stacy, it's time." I'd known the time had come, but when I saw that hawk, I knew it was time to bring this book out into the world.

Metaconscious Entrepreneur has been waiting to be birthed for a while. It's been living in my heart and soul for years. For a long time, the world wasn't ready, and I wasn't ready … but I am now. The time has finally come for us to open up to the wisdom—the deep, intense, unquestionable wisdom—about the truth of our reality and who we really are. It's the truth of our power as human beings having a spiritual experience and as spiritual beings having a human experience. The truth is simple: you have everything you need to create your world, and you've had it all along.

So, what do I mean by *creating your world*? Well, you have what it takes to build a business that generates unimaginable wealth while changing the world. You just didn't know it yet! I'm guessing somewhere deep in your soul, you've been waiting for inspiration, and that's why you chose this book. You've been waiting for a path that leads to a deeper, stronger connection to yourself. You've been searching for a new way of growing a business and creating conscious wealth. You've been searching for a new way of being an entrepreneur who can create opportunity, fulfillment, joy, and abundance on an *exponential* level, and the good news is you're exactly where you should be because if you let it, this book will guide you there.

Introduction

Metaconscious Entrepreneur, Defined

If you look around, you'll see that the old ways of doing business are disappearing. The old ways of "me against you" and "competition over collaboration" are dying because pushy marketing and sales tactics based on fear, scarcity, and pain points just aren't working anymore. And in this moment in time—where the old is not yet dead and the new is yet to fully bloom—a new tribe of entrepreneurs is beginning to rise. These are revolutionary small business owners, company leaders, CEOs, and solopreneurs. They're people from every gender, race, and nationality, and they know they're ready to forge a new path to doing business.

They're hungry for insights and techniques that work on a strategic level and in the unseen world of energy. They know that we are all ultimately one, no matter who we are or where we come from. They know that we belong to an infinite tapestry of existence that is hard to understand on a conscious level, but it resonates with our awakened hearts and souls. These entrepreneurs have a burning, all-consuming desire to start, grow, and scale a successful business *without* sacrificing their mental, physical, and emotional well-being. This is a transformational, rebellious, wildly different breed of trailblazers, paradigm-shifters, and world-changers. They're metaconscious entrepreneurs, and if you were drawn to this book, so are you.

You *don't* resonate with traditional marketing and sales methods that are predominantly focused on "what's in it for me" because you're about "what's in it for *we*," and you're about to learn how to implement potent, effective ways to grow a remarkably successful business that makes a positive, purposeful difference. You'll learn to create abundance and ultimately do the work you know you are here to do in the world—work that contributes to the betterment of all whose lives you touch. I want you to think of *Metaconscious Entrepreneur* as your personal go-to manual of rebellious wisdom. It's the "underground guide" for a secret society of covert business operatives who are changing the rules and changing the world at the same time, and you can turn to it again and again for guidance and support as you work with the new rules of starting and growing a conscious business.

As you journey through these pages, don't be surprised if you begin to feel immersed in gratitude, love, creativity, bliss, and abundance because those are the energies I've infused into these words, and that's the message I'm here to share. These emotions are your natural state of being, and it's what you will experience more and more as you step into becoming a metaconscious entrepreneur on the leading edge of the next evolution of business and entrepreneurship. I've been called to tap deeply into the truth of where we are on this revolutionary path to abundance for all, and I'm here to share the truth of our reality, the truth of our power, the truth of who we really are, and the truth of how simple it can be to change the world and tip the balance so the good gals (and guys) get to win. You're about to uncover unexpected ideas in business and marketing and sales that will replace the tired, outdated ways of competition, hustle, and scarcity.

Imagine creating your personal heaven on earth while transforming the world of business and transforming the whole world at the same time? Imagine if you could understand exactly how to connect with, access, communicate with, and tap into the power of God/Source/Universe (GUS) at *will* to create magic and miracles in your life and business while simultaneously keeping your feet firmly on the ground as a human being. What could you do with this knowledge? *Metaconscious Entrepreneur* has the answers.

You're a conscious, spiritual being, but that doesn't mean you have to miss out on the fullest, juiciest experiences this human life has to offer, including achieving massive goals as you create abundance in your business as a metaconscious entrepreneur. So, how do you experience both worlds? How do you experience life as an infinite spiritual being who's tapped into divine inner bliss and contentment—those powerful intangible, energetic states that material things can't give us—and experience the physical world as an empowered human? How do you stay connected to the unknowable, omnipotent, omnipresent loving energy of GUS and still stay grounded as you experience all the joy and the beauty of this magnificent playground we call Earth? The simple answer is *balance*.

It's about finding that balance as you walk in the spiritual world *and* the material world with grace, and it's about calling in everything you want on this physical plane and *not* being attached to any of it. Things start to get screwed up when we pursue external things—stuff—to fulfill heart-level desires like love, peace, a sense of belonging, and all of those needs we have as human beings. Any time we believe an outside goal is the thing that will guide us to fulfill our innermost needs, we'll end up disappointed, disheartened, and disillusioned. When we blindly follow external goals—when we're blindly on the path to bigger, brighter, better, and faster—what we're really doing is going down a rabbit hole where we get stuck in the seeking, but we never get to the finding.

The truth is our internal needs, our spiritual needs, can be attained in the easiest way imaginable: simply by remembering the truth of our soul. We all have what it takes to tap into the power and potential of the present moment, and we all have what it takes to connect with GUS in every moment, to cocreate anything and everything we can possibly imagine.

Why I Wrote This Book

This book is a conscious call to arms because the world needs a new way forward. Now is the time for positive advances, methods, and ways of living, being, doing, loving, working, and learning to come through and transform all of our broken systems from government to politics, to education, to health, to industry and finance ... every damn thing under the sun! But first, I have a confession. I didn't always believe in doing things differently and in finding my own way, my own path. I didn't always listen to my intuition and my inner guidance. I spent years (and thousands of dollars) seeking the truth outside of myself and looking for answers and solutions for my business from gurus, teachers, and experts who knew nothing about me and what my heart longed for. I used to be a personal growth and business development junkie, and my addiction was out of control.

There was a point in my life when I pretty much *inhaled* self-help books and books on marketing and sales plus courses and programs on getting to that elusive "seven-figure" status in my business, and I went after it like it was the air that I breathed. I never stopped searching for the next hit, the next fix, and the next idea that would change me and make me a better entrepreneur and a better human being. I was looking for the solution that would finally "fix" me and finally "fix" my business. In the process, I became a speed reader and then a "speed action-taker," implementing tactics, techniques, methodologies, and mantras at dizzying speeds. However, no matter how much I read and how fast I tried to keep up, I couldn't escape the feeling that something was *missing*.

After years of chasing improvement, enhancement, and *perfection*, I realized something profound. My intention—my insatiable hunger—for personal and business growth didn't arise from a deep desire to be better that I was before. It came from fear—a fear of failure and a fear of imperfection. This fear was overwhelming, and it continued to grow because deep down,

I believed I was not *doing* enough or *being* enough. When this realization hit me, I looked around and noticed the cost of my drive and my ambition. I'd lost time with the ones I love the most, and it was time I could never get back. I was exhausted and depleted to the core because of a punishing schedule that left no room for dreaming. There was only room for doing. I finally decided "enough is enough." I decided to go down a different route and take a different path—a path that overrode my need to prove to myself that I was worthy and that I deserved love, happiness, and success. It was a path that spoke to my soul, and I learned so much along the way.

When you discover how to drop within and listen to your intuition—the innate wisdom and guidance embedded in your soul—you start to tap into the *field of infinite creation*. This is the field of *all* possibilities. This is the energetic space where your limitless potential and your higher self meet. This is the place where miracles happen and where *impossible* simply doesn't exist. It's the place where you receive signs, insights, opportunities, and everything else you need to get to where you want to go in your business and in your life. And when you have the courage to trust in what you receive and take action, one step at a time, one foot in front of another, that's when you'll come up with business ideas that didn't even exist before—and that's when you get to experience mind-blowing growth and expansion with hardly any effort.

We're already starting to see glimpses of this happening around the world with people who are tapped into the field of infinite creation and following through with the insights and ideas that they receive. We're seeing new inventions and innovations and new socially conscious companies like Patagonia and TOMS breaking the mold of how business is done. Can you imagine what will happen when more and more of these new creations start coming through? Can you imagine what will be possible for our world?

There's something you need to know about me as we journey through this book together. I see *everything* as being part of an energetic framework. I see everything through an energetic lens. I can tune in to the energy and see what's *really* going on beneath the surface and what needs to be done to create, manifest, build, and grow the business you are here to create.

I can clearly see the vision and the pathway that will get us to a brand-new way of being ... people like you and me, people who care, people who want to let go of the systems and methods of business and life that are damaged and damaging so we can all move into a powerful, inclusive, compassionate and wildly successful new world.

How This Book Will Benefit You

This book is perfect if you've been around the business and self-help block once, twice, three times, or more. We've studied, we've read, and we've implemented, and now we're craving the next level of evolution. We're craving the next level of understanding of what *this*—this life, this reality, this system of making a living—is really all about. We want deeper purpose, deeper connection, and deeper truths that are also grounded in reality and can be translated into everyday human experiences.

Throughout this book, I'll be showing you how to beautifully balance the physical realm and the nonphysical realm, and you'll be learning how to bring the nonphysical into the physical and the physical into the nonphysical—what's commonly known as co-creation or manifestation—but in a much more meaningful way than just manifesting things like cars and mansions and holidays. There's nothing wrong with any of that, and you'll learn how to consistently and accurately manifest those types of things. You'll also learn to create so much more than that on the energetic plane.

I've categorized *Metaconscious Entrepreneur* into three potent segments or truths: the truth about consciousness and energy, the truth about conscious success and abundance, the truth about accelerated growth in conscious business.

The truth about consciousness and energy introduces the unbreakable laws or precepts of energy that you must understand as part of your foundational knowledge. The truth about conscious success and abundance reveals the three codes—the awareness code, the alignment code, and the awaken code—you need to unlock success and abundance on a remarkable scale and in ways that bring maximum benefit to you, your business, your team, your clients, your customers, and everyone you connect with. Finally, we have the truth about accelerated growth in conscious business that uncovers high conscious business rules. These rules are like tools in your metaconscious tool kit as you navigate new territory and begin growing a prosperous, conscious business that serves you and serves the world at the same time. These three truths fit together like puzzle pieces, and when you work with them and apply the wisdom and strategy behind each one, there is literally no end to the material, physical, emotional, and spiritual wealth and abundance you can create in your life and business.

I want you to think of *Metaconscious Entrepreneur* as a map or blueprint to having it all, and I don't mean having it all in ways that only feel good in the moment or having it all in ways that ask for sacrifice where you end up putting yourself last on your own priority list. *Metaconscious Entrepreneur* is for you if you're just starting out because it's about finding a powerful, meaningful path to building a business that lets you enjoy the world with all of its glorious offerings and also experience a sense of sacred contentment within because you know you're living a meaningful life.

This book is also for you if you're already at the point where you're seen as a massive success in the material world. You've hit most or all of your financial and other external goals, and you keep raising the bar on yourself because you're not really feeling any of it in your heart. It all feels a little bit empty and maybe even meaningless, but you push yourself even harder because now you're feeling guilty. Shouldn't you be more grateful for what you have? Shouldn't you be feeling fulfilled and happy? You can't stop asking yourself these questions, but since you have no answers, you keep doing what you've always done.

You keep on following the accepted path ... the one everyone says you should follow. You keep working hard, and you keep playing hard. You know meditation and exercise are good for you, so you do both of those things every day. You try to eat right and say the right things in every single moment, but the harder you try, the worse it gets. You can't ignore that feeling deep in your heart. You yearn for something more, something better, something deeper than just doing everything perfectly and getting everything right.

What This Book Is Truly About

You're a pioneer. You wouldn't be attracted to this book, and you wouldn't be reading these words if you weren't. It's time to let your power be felt and be seen so you can truly impact the world in every imaginable way and also in ways that you've never dared to imagine. The world needs you to be tapped into what's already within you so you can receive ideas, insights, innovations, and inspirations that can take the entire human race out of the kind of thinking that breaks us down and finally embrace the kind of thinking that breaks us through. We need loving leaders—loving metaconscious entrepreneurs—like you. We need people who will raise us up and out of the restrictive, conventional, small, suppressive social and cultural beliefs, thoughts, and ideologies that have shattered millions of lives and brought the world to its knees. That's what this book is *truly* about.

It's about entrepreneurship, business, and wealth, but it's also about so much more. It's about a pathway I've uncovered through divine guidance, my own studies, my own life experiences, and the experiences of thousands of clients and students. You'll find yourself opening up to the field of infinite creation, which is where all things are connected, where all things are created, and where you are living your life full-on and full-out, being fully you as you enter an out-of-this-world spiritual experience *and* human experience!

This isn't about *learning* as much as it is about *remembering*. You're reading these words to *remember* your soul, to *remember* who you *really* are, and to awaken to your power. It's no wonder so many of us were infatuated with the Wizard of Oz when we were little. So much of that story relates to who we truly are. Dorothy wonders, *Was it all just a dream?* My question is this: Was it just a dream—or was she *remembering* who she really was? It turns out Glenda the Good Witch was right when she said, "You've had the power all along, my dear." Click, click, click. Home sweet home. Land of magic. Land of light. Land of dark. Land of illusions. Land of truth. Home in our hearts. Home in our souls.

So, welcome home. This is your time. It's time to remember who you really are and what you're truly capable of doing, having, and being. You've had the power all along, and now it's time to reconnect to it and use it to change your inner world and then your outer world manifestations and make some powerful positive waves while you do it!

I'm deeply grateful to walk this path beside you as I continue to evolve and shift in my own consciousness, knowing that everything is energy. When we master our energy, we master our lives. When we master our lives, we change the world, and that is where our story and our journey together begin. We're starting with energy and what it means, why it matters, and how it works as the secret, invisible master key that unlocks the door to *everything*. Come, take my hand … let's do this!

PART I

THE TRUTH ABOUT CONSCIOUSNESS AND ENERGY

CHAPTER 1

The First Precept: Everything Is Energy

Mr. Chalmers abruptly threw his fists down on the desk and yelled, "Everything is moving, shifting, and vibrating because *everything* is energy!" He picked up a pen and brandished it at the roomful of stunned fifteen-year-olds staring up at him. "This is not what it appears to be. It's moving energy!"

Tenth-grade chemistry was my first introduction to the science of how the world operates beneath the surface and in the spaces that are invisible to the human eye. I can't remember much of middle school or high school; it's all just beyond the reach of my conscious mind. It's somewhere on the edges of my memory. What's wild is that out of my entire high school career, that image of Mr. Chalmers standing there with his pen remains clear and bright as day. That memory never left me, and over the years, it's resurfaced again and again. For the longest time, I didn't know why, but I do now.

The universe knew that my path was to understand how to work with energy and teach it to the world *decades* before I did. I despised science, but that lesson with Mr. Chalmers embedded in my subconscious kept showing up in other areas of my life: my grandmother being obsessed with things like biorhythms and spirituality that reached far beyond my Catholic upbringing, believing my stuffed animals were alive and able to have full conversations with me since I was five, and finding a coach-training program that was 100 percent based on consciousness principles and energy leadership.

As I look back and connect the dots, I can see that, deep down, I somehow knew I was put on this earth to teach and to share about energy, about consciousness, and about the infinite nature of our true power. I didn't realize the depth of this calling until just recently, but it's the message and movement that I am destined to live and breathe.

I'm here to share the truth with metaconscious entrepreneurs everywhere, the geniuses, the paradigm shifters, the ones who are hiding in plain sight. They're loving leaders, game-changing innovators, and master manifesters. They are change agents who have a crucial mission on our planet right now—old souls who are ready to return to our power and our deep knowing. And make no mistake—they're here to shake things up, and I count myself as one among them!

I see us as part of the next evolution in consciousness, and we are witnessing the tipping point of human evolution on earth. The entire world is about to shift from a predominantly catabolic state where we're in a negative, destructive, energetic state to a predominantly anabolic state where we're in a positive, constructive, energetic state. This tiny, one-degree tilt will quantum leap humankind and put us light years ahead of where we are now in every possible way.

Given that everything is energy, it makes perfect sense that energy itself is where this evolution begins. It's the entry point to consciousness, and it's the entry point to the field of infinite creation. So, let's look at what energy actually *is*. These are what I like to call the seven universal principles of energy. The entire universe operates on these seven principles:

- Principle 1: All energy has a vibration.
- Principle 2: All energy has a frequency.
- Principle 3: All energy is either life-enhancing or life-depleting—it is either catabolic or anabolic energy.
- Principle 4: All energy exists in the field of infinite creation.

- Principle 5: Like energy attracts like energy, which is known as the law of attraction.
- Principle 6: Energy can't be created or destroyed; it can only be transformed.
- Principle 7: High-frequency energy or a positive energetic state in a single individual has the power to counterbalance low energetic states in countless others.

When Einstein discovered that "matter is energy," he opened the door to merging science and metaphysics. Scientists have shown that energy cannot die; it can only transform. And by its very nature, energy must go forward or backward; it cannot stand still.

You are energy. Your skin, which appears solid, is trillions of swiftly moving molecules orbiting each other at a specific vibrational rate. It is a physical life rate you have earned in the past because of how harmoniously or disharmoniously you have lived your life up until this moment. When you are harmonious for a lifetime, you will have attained the highest vibrational rate—the GUS/field of infinite creation level—where you become the master manifester and co-creator of your life and business. All ideas, desires, and goals can enter your reality in an instant.

CHAPTER 2

The Second Precept: You Are Whole and Complete Now and Always

The field of infinite creation is where all energy and potential exist. This is the field of instant manifestations and of desires coming to life in the time it takes to think a single thought or feel an emotion. No matter who you are or where you come from, no matter what you've accomplished or not accomplished in your life or business, you have access to this field, and it is always available to you. There are zero exceptions to this precept.

Connecting to the field of infinite creation begins with remembering who you truly are and knowing that you have infinite power to cocreate anything and everything you desire. This isn't about learning, it isn't about changing, and it isn't about anything other than remembering. It begins when you let go of the need to stay busy, to fit in, to be praised, to go along to get along, to seek approval, or to seek validation.

- It begins when you let go of chasing your tail.
- It begins when you let go of feeling like you can't keep up.
- It begins when you let go of feeling guilty.
- It begins when you let go of *not* being in ten places at once.

Remembering is about liberating yourself from the shackles that hold you back and hold you down. You realize the shackles are of other people's expectations, other people's opinions of what you should and should not do, and other people's definitions of what success should look like for you in your business.

This remembering didn't happen for me for a long time, but I finally remembered. I was driving home from an intensive weekend retreat where I'd been meditating and reflecting on a lot of the knowledge that is in this book. I was suddenly immersed in an overwhelmingly beautiful, awe-inspiring emotion. It was unconditional love. It was bliss. It was peace. It was excitement. It was trust. It was all of that and more. It felt spiritual and sacred and holy and completely healing. I had never felt that way before, and it moved me in a way I'll never forget. It felt like I was receiving a message from love itself, from life itself. I remember saying out loud, "This is me, and I am home."

In that moment, I could feel my soul, and I could feel the immense vastness of my power. I was invincible and fearless. I knew that I was eternally supported, accepted, embraced, and loved for just being alive, and it had nothing to do with doing, trying, or seeking. It had nothing to do with achievements, accomplishments, or goals. As I leaned into that feeling, and as I basked in the healing and knowledge of the experience of remembering, I finally and irrevocably understood that I am already whole. I am already complete. I finally realized I'd been looking for myself in all the wrong places. I'd been looking for me *outside* of myself.

Before that moment, I'd climbed the career ladder, and I was always up for doing more, being more, and trying harder. It was so important to me that other people recognized and acknowledged that I was a good mom, a good daughter, a good friend, and a good wife. So, I kept pushing and striving. I had experienced a lot of material success—and I'm grateful for all that I have in my life—but I was also exhausted and depleted because no matter what I had or what I achieved, it was never enough.

My gratitude, my inner peace, and my sense of accomplishment were always short-lived. Sometimes those good feelings lasted just a few seconds before my mind did the thing it had been trained to do. And that was to ask, What's next? Again and again, like a broken record. The only way to get it to stop was to go off looking for the next goal, the next target, or the next win because it felt like "the next thing" would finally bring me home to myself. Until that day of remembering that nothing outside of us can make us whole or bring us home, that we are already whole and complete, that we are a part of the tapestry of all things—the field of infinite creation. I remember, and now it's time for you to remember too.

It's time for you to remember so you can get out of the rat race and free yourself from the bottomless pit of seeking wholeness outside of yourself. Whether that means through personal development, through more flaws that need to be fixed, through more achievements that need to be added to your resume, through more letters behind your name, through becoming sexier, or thinner, or faster, or whatever it happens to be for you.

When you remember this truth about who you are, when you align with it, and when you stop looking outside for what can only be found inside, you experience the highest levels of freedom, joy, passion, consciousness, and love. And that's when you are the closest the field of infinite creation, where all things are created and materialized for your human experience. This includes everything that happens in your work and in your business.

So, this is your moment. This is your moment to remember. I know that even as you're reading these words, and hearing them in your mind, something in your soul already knows it and already recognizes it. It's unchangeable, which is what makes it true.

If your conscious mind is saying, "That's way too woo-woo," or you happen to have a ton of thoughts and questions rushing through your mind like, "But what about?" or "How does this work?" or "It doesn't sound logical," or whatever excuses your literal, sequential left-brain is coming with up right now, know that it's just old patterning and old ways of being. I invite you to just sit in the message of this precept that you were created whole and complete, and that you, me, and every single human on the planet has the power to create anything and everything from the field of infinite creation because we are not just part of the field; we *are* the field.

When we awaken to this forgotten reality of who we are, when we begin to embody it and live it from deep within every cell of our physical being and from every aspect of our souls, the field will be as close as our breath and manifestation, and co-creation will feel as natural as breathing.

CHAPTER 3

The Third Precept: You Can Instantly Bring Your Desires into Your reality

The art of effortless manifestation begins with embodying the previous precept: we are not just a part of the field of infinite creation; we *are* the field. It's about bringing our consciousness back to our original state of innate wholeness and infinite power.

It is this consciousness that shapes our reality, and it is always at the vibrational frequency of our energy. The higher our vibrational frequency, the higher our level of consciousness and the closer we are to experiencing effortless manifestation from the field of infinite creation. So, how do you attain higher levels of vibrational frequency? Start with your intention.

You can access the field of infinite creation and instantly bring your desires into your reality in your life and business when you create, mold, and shape your experience, moment by moment, with conscious intention and choice (you'll discover exactly how to do this with the eighth precept). It's about bringing the power of mindful awareness to your energy levels, thoughts, and beliefs in every moment of your life experience and tapping into the power of choice as you design your day-to-day life with intentional purpose.

Energy and vibrational frequency are solidified and clarified through intention. Your intention gets your energy focused and clear, and it has the power to drive your vibrational frequency up (or down as the case may be). Living with intention heightens, strengthens, and intensifies your natural ability to connect with the field at any moment. When you can raise your energy and your vibrational frequency, you can bring your desires into reality in a snap.

If your desire arises from feelings of lack, which vibrate at very low levels, it is *impossible* to have that desire manifest, which is why you must be aware of energetic nuances.

For most people, energetic nuances are hard to detect because they're almost imperceptible. They're tiny differences in feelings and emotions such as appreciation versus recognition or desire versus craving. These emotions seem like they're one and the same, but they're not. When you connect to yourself and become fully aware of these energetic nuances, you'll have the power to shift and change your energy and vibrational frequency levels *at will*. The result? Effortless, instant manifestation. Detecting these nuances gets easier with time; it's about recognizing the difference between how you *think* you feel and how you *really* feel.

Let's take desire versus craving. At first glance, these feelings or energies seem to be the same, but let's dive deeper. We've all experienced desire that feels like excitement and anticipation. It feels expansive, it feels light, and it feels energizing. It's like the desire you feel when you're counting down the days to Christmas morning or the desire for that upcoming dream vacation. Then there's craving that comes from a place of painful urgency. It's a hunger from a place of neediness and desperation—like when you haven't had a bite to eat all day. It feels like you're starving, and it *doesn't* feel good to be starving.

Desire is different. Desire for a delicious meal—the one you've been looking forward to all day—comes from high energy and vibrational levels. Your mouth is watering because you can't wait to dig in. On the other hand, craving food feels like starvation. You just want to wolf down anything that's on the plate in front of you. You don't savor it, and you don't enjoy it because all you're trying to do is *alleviate* your need with painful urgency.

Attaining higher levels of consciousness is about navigating energetic nuances in the moment and shifting to higher vibrational

Stacy Hartmann

frequencies with the power of choice. It's choosing desire over craving. It's choosing love over fear. It's about getting to the highest levels of consciousness, which is where you'll start to experience effortless manifestations in the field of infinite creation.

CHAPTER 4

The Fourth Precept: You Can Be 100 Percent Spiritual and 100 Percent Human at the Same Time

For most people, reaching spiritual enlightenment is about leaving everything in the physical realm behind as they detach from the material world. There's nothing wrong with that, but what if you're like me and want more? What if you want to experience the kind of deep awakening, centeredness, and joy that come from spiritual enlightenment while relishing a fully human experience at the same time?

This means you can enjoy a luxurious seven-star island retreat while experiencing unshakeable inner peace. It means you get front-row seats at a rock concert and stay immersed in every second of music, magic, and genius without feeling better than the people in the cheap seats. It means you're no longer thinking about what people are thinking about you and making all of your life and business choices from a place of empowered intuitive truth. It seems like for the longest time we've been forced to choose:

- Do I want to be spiritual—or do I want to be rich?
- Do I want to be spiritual—or do I want to be successful?
- Do I want to be spiritual—or do I just want to be human?

Here's a much better question: How do we create an enlightened spiritual-human experience? The answer is to create conscious wealth and success in every possible way, in every possible reality, in every possible experience. This is not about choosing to be spiritual over being human because, at the end of the day, we are both. I'm a human being, and I'm a spiritual being. I'm a spiritual being having a human experience, *and* I'm a human being having a spiritual experience. Have you noticed that the more you tap into the realization that you're a spiritual being, the less you let yourself enjoy a full human experience, and the more you desire a human experience, the more you feel disconnected from your spirituality? I call BS because you don't have to do that!

The truth is being 100 percent spiritual opens the door to 100 percent of your human experience, and it's in this space that you grow and thrive as a metaconscious entrepreneur. The truth is you can have it all on the spiritual and on the material realm, and you can have both at the same time. Humanity has evolved to a place in our consciousness where experiencing your life as a spiritual being and as a human being are no longer mutually exclusive. We don't have to be a recluse or a monk meditating on a mountaintop with zero attachments and nothingness just so we can experience the fullness of our spirituality.

Creating conscious wealth and success in life and business is about melding and blending our inner and outer worlds. It's about having the best of both worlds and experiencing the deepest levels of connection, love, joy, beauty, and inner peace—while co-creating physical manifestations to expand, enjoy, and fully experience our human lives.

I think of conscious wealth and success as the lovechild of Einstein and Buddha. Buddha and Buddhist philosophy apply to creating our inner world, and Einstein's theories apply to creating our outer world of energy, consciousness, matter, and bringing things into the physical realm.

If you want to dance with your spirituality and your humanity at the same time, you start with your inner world or "traditional" enlightenment. I like to call this "Enlightenment 1.0." You start with consciousness, knowing, and awareness. You start with principles like nonattachment, nonjudgment, and unconditional love (we'll explore this in chapter 9 "The Awareness Code").

From Enlightenment 1.0, we make the transition to science and the materialization of matter, and this is where the outer world and Einstein come to the table. We tap into our intuition, and we actually take action—physical action—with our feet on the ground in the direction of and in devotion to our creativity, our imagination, and our passions.

For people who are restricted to Enlightenment 1.0, there's no need for action. You can sit with your inner peace and the truth of life, and that's that. However, Enlightenment 2.0 asks for more. It's about connecting to our intuition and aligning with our passions, creativity, and hearts to squeeze the fullest experience that we possibly can have in this human existence and to truly create an outer world that matches an enlightened inner world.

So, what would an outer world that matches an enlightened inner world look like? It would look like everybody's needs are provided for. It would look like conflict eradicated. It would look like collaboration instead of competition in business, and while we can still enjoy competing, *how and why* we compete will be totally different. It would be for our expansion of the human experience and not to win because we're "better than" or to take somebody else's power away. I believe building conscious businesses is one of the fastest ways to create this new reality. Entrepreneurs who embrace Enlightenment 2.0 will quickly create a conscious business that leads to a beautiful, aligned outer world.

In this world, there is heartfelt acceptance of all races, all genders, and all people.

It is a world of peace, harmony, and abundance for all. It is a world of unconditional, unquestionable, and everlasting love.

CHAPTER 5

The Fifth Precept: Effort is Limited. Energy is Limitless.

Imagine you're out at sea in a rowboat on a beautiful day. The sun is shining, and the sky is blue. Then, without warning, thunderclouds block out the sun. You know a storm is coming. You can see the shore, and you know you need to get there sooner rather than later. So, you throw both oars into the ocean and start to paddle with your hands. It sounds nuts, but that's what we do all the damn time in life and in business. We have these oars—the tools—to help us get through challenges and obstacles. These oars can help us get to where we want to go with very little effort—sometimes with no effort at all—but we throw those game-changing, live-saving oars into the sea and decide we want to paddle with our hands. So, we work and hustle and push and keep going and doing whatever it takes to move forward.

And when you believe it's all on you to "make s#it happen," what's really happening is that you're ignoring the oars—the most potent tool you have. It's a limitless resource. I'm talking about the endless flow of energy that's available to you in every second of every day.

Here's the thing; we've all received messages and memes about entrepreneurship and success. We all read the memos. You've gotta *hustle*. You've gotta make it work. You've got to take action now—or you're gonna miss the boat. Great advice, right? Wrong.

The truth is we're addicted to *hard*. We're addicted to *complicated*. We're addicted to what I call "efforting," and if it's not difficult, it's not worth doing. That's the story we tell ourselves, and we've been fed this story from way back when we were little kids. We can only access a fraction of our potential as a limitless, energetic being through efforting as opposed to tapping into the world of energy and leveraging that to kick-start exponential progress. That's when you start to see the magic of divine orchestration and synchronistic grid and the power of the field of infinite creation come into play, and that is so much higher and grander and more graceful than anything we can create or make happen through human effort alone.

So, how do you do that? How do you tap into the energy of the field or GUS? The trick is to sustain and contain and focus your energy toward one thing at a time and then release expectations of *how* it's going to happen.

For instance, let's imagine you're thinking of growing your client or customer base in your business, and you have five steps you need to take to make that happen. The secret is to leverage the limitless energy of the field of infinite creation to bring all your attention, intention, and focus to that first step in the moment. Most people unknowingly disperse, scatter, and fragment their focus into multiple directions. They keep thinking about steps 2 through 5 even before they work on step 1. Then they start to think about what could go wrong, which kills the energy and scatters it. That's what efforting looks like.

When you work with limitless energy, you'll set a strong intention for only step 1. So, when we focus all the energy on a powerful experience and set a strong intention for only the first step, then the likelihood of the second, third, fourth and fifth steps happening exactly the way you want them to—or even better— through synchronistic opportunities and magical "coincidences" is a thousand times greater than if you're fragmenting your intention, attention, and focus to address all five of the steps.

Your key job is to create the big vision and tap into the essence of it. See the vision of your desires so clearly in your imagination that you start to feel the emotion swelling up inside of you. This creates a magnetic vortex of attraction. Forget about the how, which is really about being detached from the how, to allow for the energy of GUS or the infinite field of creation to orchestrate the details and steps it will unfold. This will guide you to effortlessly flow along the path to manifesting the big vision. Your biggest, brightest visions and dreams and goals are not going to arise from the effort. They are going to manifest when you show up, fully present to the genius of the energy at play, in a way that feels authentic to you.

So, it's like we don't want to just see a path. We don't want to figure out a straight-line path because the minute we see a straight-line path, we pretty much screw ourselves because we've just cut off any and all other possibilities that could enter that path because we're so streamlined and thinking this is the path—and this is where we're going.

Effort will always be limited because, at the end of the day, effort is restricted by elements like time and physical, human energy. Let's face it. There are only so many hours in a day and only so long that you can keep working before you fall asleep at your desk because of sheer exhaustion. So, if you happen to have big dreams, if you want to manifest a massive, world-changing vision for your business, you need to tap into something more than human effort, and that's the limitless energy of the field of infinite creation where all possibilities exist.

CHAPTER 6

The Sixth Precept: Time Is an Illusion. You Have the Power to Slow it Down or Speed it Up Past, Present, and Future.

Time influences all things, and our view of time—what it is and how it works—is the biggest block in our journey to abundance, success, fulfillment, and joy. The truth is time is not what we were taught, and if you want to have power and control over time, you must examine your relationship and unpack your beliefs and blocks about time. Let's start by looking at common beliefs about time and how it works:

1. Time is finite.
2. Time moves sequentially.
3. Time is non-replenishable.

In the grounded world of physical form, time appears finite because all that lives must die. There is an end. There comes a day when we run out of tomorrows. This is true in the physical world—the world of the seen—but in the world of energy and instant manifestations, in the field of infinite creation, there is no beginning and no end because we are infinite beings who come from GUS. In our purest form, there is no death or birth. We are pure energy that morphs and changes and transforms in every moment (see chapter 1, "Everything is Energy")

In the world of the seen, time seems to move sequentially—day follows night, night follows day, and seasons come and go. It all happens in perfect order again and again and again, through millennia. However, that's not how it works in the field of infinite creation, which is where we live and manifest and cocreate as metaconscious entrepreneurs. Einstein said, "The distinction between past, present, and future is a stubbornly held illusion."

Quantum physicists believe in timelessness. There is no passage of time; there is only a kind of continuous flow that encompasses the past, present, and future, which is known as the space-time continuum. This view is the opposite of the principles of quantum mechanics, which is where time is believed to be sequential with a past that has gone, the present that is happening now, and a future that is yet to come.

The field of infinite creation is in alignment with quantum physics and exists in a timeless state that encompasses all of time—all at the same time. This means that at any moment, you can step into a different reality. This is the foundational nature and magic of the field of infinite creation where instant manifestations take place.

In the material world, time is a non-replenishable resource, but in the field of infinite creation, time is limitless and continuous. Time is endless, which literally means there is no end. There is an infinite amount of time available to each of us. Viewed through the lens of quantum physics, GUS, and the field of infinite creation, time as we think we know it does not exist. It is an illusion, and the true nature of time is elastic. It can be stretched to speed up and slow down based on our personal experiences and observations of how time passes, and the tool that we can use to do this is *presence*.

Present moment awareness is the key to *time control*. As highlighted by master spiritual teacher Eckhart Tolle in his global bestseller *The Power of Now*, the power of the present has no limits. In simple terms, presence stretches time. Presence slows down time, and where there is presence, there is spaciousness in the heart, mind, and inner world. This spaciousness dissolves and collapses time.

In other words, you bring your consciousness into the present to slow down or speed up time, and you work with creating spaciousness in consciousness to open yourself up to receiving unexpected ideas and intuitive hits that will let you leap ahead in your journey toward your goal—whether that's financial freedom, creating a new service or offer in your business, or learning how to play the violin.

One of the most powerful ways to train the mind in both presence and spaciousness is through meditation. Most people think of meditation as the "emptying of the mind," but I have a different take. I see meditation as an *active* experience, and this is why I love to take walking meditations and lose myself in dancing meditations. I meditate in my writing and journaling. I meditate while working with coaching clients.

Present moment meditation rather than emptying has to do with focusing and lasering in. This is about funneling your attention and bringing all of your focus to the one thing in front of you, and it's the ultimate "one thing at a time" experience. So, if you're in a conversation, it's about listening with your whole body, fully and completely. If you're writing, it's about bringing your energy and focus to the words on the page and nothing else. If you're dancing, it's about immersing yourself in the music. In this way, there is no past, and there is no future. There is only now, and in that now, there are infinite possibilities because the field of infinite creation can only exist in the now.

CHAPTER 7

The Seventh Precept: Your Level of Consciousness Creates Your Reality

Something incredible is happening even as you read these words—your consciousness is creating your reality moment by moment, and it *never* stops. Your consciousness is essentially your internal energetic state, and it's made up of everything you think, feel, and believe. All of this creates your external world, and this includes anything and everything that happens in your immediate experience and environment. From your experience at the DMV to how many new clients or customers you see in your business at any given time, your external world is shaped by your internal energetic state. The sooner you accept that everything you experience out in the world is a direct result of your own consciousness or energetic state, the sooner you get to cocreate your life and your business.

But what about when things go wrong? Your product launch fails and only one person buys, your potential client says "no" at the last minute, or your make a bad investment in your business. Does this mean you're the one creating this crappy stuff in your business? The short answer is no.

While the seventh precept—your level of consciousness creates your reality—is always true, it doesn't mean that the negative, icky, unwanted stuff that happens is your fault. Your consciousness continues to shape your reality—whether you're aware of it or not—and when negative things happen, it just means you were unaware of where your consciousness was at the time, and it's time to shift into higher levels of consciousness, which is where the seven levels of consciousness come in.

The seven levels of consciousness are like an energetic scale or dial, and I've interpreted them based on the work of Bruce Schneider, founder of the Institute for Professional Excellence in Coaching (iPEC) and Dr. David Hawkins, the spiritual teacher and best-selling author of *The Map of Consciousness Explained*. You can work with the seven levels of consciousness to shift and change your internal state from lower energetic states like fear or doubt to higher states like enthusiasm and joy.

Understanding each level and turning the dial up and down puts *all* the power in your hands. It lets you overcome self-sabotage, procrastination, self-doubt, fear, anxiety, and just about every other block, limiting belief, thought, or emotion that holds you back from creating what you desire in your business and your life. Before we dive deeper into the seven levels, what they are, and how to move up to higher levels, you need to know the simple system or lens that will help you identify where you are on the scale. I call this the *Triple A Manifestation Method* or AAA: awareness, acceptance, and action.

AAA is about identifying your energetic state or where you land on the seven levels of consciousness. Bringing awareness to your energetic state is especially helpful when you're experiencing resistance. For instance, if you have resistance around things like presenting on stage, engaging on social media, or having sales conversations with potential clients, the first "A" in the AAA manifestation method will give you the clarity you need to take charge of your energetic state.

Awareness instantly shines a spotlight on where you are on the seven levels of consciousness so you can start to shift your energy in a way that will support you so you can achieve the outcome you desire. Awareness is accessible through the energy of truth, and stepping into awareness is as simple as asking and honestly answering this question: What level of consciousness am I at right now?

Once you've identified your level of consciousness, you're ready to move on to the second A, acceptance, and this is about *first* being okay with wherever you happen to be on the seven levels of consciousness scale. So, here's the thing ... a lot of conscious, loving people feel like they've let themselves down or let others down because they're not switched on 100 percent of the time. They feel like they need incredibly high levels of consciousness pretty much all the time. This is absolutely not true, and it can even be damaging.

Pushing yourself to raise your energetic state and stay positive all the time can—*and will*—trigger self-judgment and self-criticism, which will quickly send you spiraling down to the lowest levels of consciousness. The antidote to this downward spiral is acceptance.

Acceptance in this context isn't about "rolling over and accepting what happens without question." This is an empowered acceptance that I'm talking about, and it's where you acknowledge what you feel, how you feel, your thoughts, and your experiences in the moment without making yourself wrong. You're curious and open to what's going on inside, and you hold space for all of it with zero judgments and criticisms.

Empowered acceptance quickly dissolves self-judgment and self-criticism, which perpetuate lower-level energies and keep you stuck on the lowest levels of consciousness. Acceptance also makes room for inner spaciousness and presence to unfold so magical inspirations, ideas, and manifestations can flow through (see chapter 6, "The Sixth Precept").

You can step into empowered acceptance by tapping into the energy of curiosity. The next time you feel yourself spiraling down into lower energetic states, say to yourself: "It's so interesting that I'm experiencing this feeling/thought/energetic state right now. I wonder what it's trying to tell me. I wonder how long it might last. I wonder what higher energetic states would feel like right now—even with the current happenings."

Finally, we have the third A in the AAA Manifestation Method, and it's where the rubber meets the road. Awareness and acceptance work on the invisible plane of energy: consciousness. Action is about real-world results. Think of action as the channel that guides manifestations from the intangible into the tangible. Action is the mode through which all energy must travel to bring through the fruits of your energetic efforts.

Action is also a powerful tool to transform lower energetic states like doubt, confusion, and fear into higher energetic states like focus, excitement, and joy, and it is fundamentally fueled by the energy of decision. You can begin to motivate action with this question: "What's the most powerful, aligned action I can take right to create the outcome I desire?"

Even if you're uncertain of the answer, action itself can give you the clarity you need to take the next step and the next and the next. Action is the magical elixir and the solution to getting the energy to flow in your business so you can leapfrog into the highest levels of consciousness, which is where instant manifestations and energetic transformations can happen.

CHAPTER 8

Understanding the Seven Levels of Consciousness

So many spiritual and metaphysical gurus and belief systems are about ditching "negative, low-vibration energies" so you can quickly get to "positive, high-vibration energies," but that's not how we roll here! The seven levels of consciousness offer an incredibly precise yet simple path to creating a life and business experience that is in absolute alignment with your values, dreams, and desires. All seven levels serve an important purpose in your journey to becoming a metaconscious entrepreneur, including the lowest levels on the scale.

Being a metaconscious entrepreneur is about embracing your spiritual self *and* your human self. We're not about denying or resisting our human condition, which means you have the space to fully accept experiences and emotions that don't necessarily feel good or comfortable in the moment.

When you bring your awareness and attention to all seven levels of consciousness, you'll know when and how to skillfully shift up and down the scale with focused intention. This gives you immense freedom and the power to shape your reality because you'll be operating from *cause* instead of *effect*. Taking action and making decisions from cause lets you respond with clarity and purpose in your business as opposed to reacting to what's going on in the heat of the moment.

When you understand the seven levels of consciousness, you'll understand how to turn the dial and change *what* you're experiencing and *how* you're experiencing every moment. You'll also learn actionable strategies you can use to hit the higher levels of consciousness so you can instantly level up your energy whenever you want to. Buckle up because this is going to be a life-changing, game-changing, *everything*-changing ride.

Level 1 Consciousness: Survive

Entrepreneurship is one of the most amazing experiences you can ever hope to have, but it's also one of the most stressful, especially at the start. So, if you're just starting out in your business, you're probably resonating at level 1 energy.

This level is called survive because survival is the only thing that's relevant or important here. The core experience at level 1 is *not dying* because when you're at this stage of consciousness, it feels like everything is a threat—and everything is about the life or death of your business. When you're immersed in level 1 consciousness, you're doing whatever needs to be done to keep your head above water, and your primary feelings are stuckness, confusion, procrastination, overwhelm, worry, and anxiety.

Entrepreneurs at level 1 are constantly playing the what-if game:

- What if I make a mistake?
- What if no one buys my stuff?
- What if I run out of money?
- What if I fail?

When the what-if playlist is on full blast in their heads, everything in business and everything about being an entrepreneur starts to take on this scary do-or-die energy. You feel like you're playing for your life even though you *know* you are physically safe.

Shifting Up from Level 1

The most effective way to move up from level 1 is to focus on the present moment, which is the only place where life takes place.

The good news is you don't have to meditate for thousands of hours or become an ordained monk to cultivate present moment awareness. It happens easily and naturally when you give yourself permission to let go of the past along with the mistakes, missed opportunities, and outcomes that didn't turn out the way you wanted them to.

Another great way to boost yourself out of level 1 is to let go of people who are in a constant state of negativity. You'll know you're in the wrong crowd when you walk away from a conversation or get-together feeling drained and miserable. Like energy attracts like energy, and when you're surrounded by people who live in denial, resistance, and scarcity—or judgmental and critical people—you'll attract more negative people and more negative energy, which only pushes you deeper into level 1.

Shifting out of level 1 also means taking better care of yourself in all areas of your being: your mental, emotional, physical, and spiritual aspects. Embody your true worth by going deeper into self-care than ever before. Be bold. Start thinking about yourself first.

Reflect on your wants, needs, and desires—and do whatever you need to do to give yourself the message that you are worthy because of who you are right this moment. You are an amazing manifestation of the divine, and since there is only one you who will ever exist in all of time, treat yourself like the brilliant one-of-a-kind treasure that you are. Whether that's choosing luxury chocolate over a cheap bar, spending time with people who lift you up, or investing in support in your business from day 1, take every opportunity to take care of yourself so you can get out of survival mode.

If you can recognize that you're in level 1 right now, know that it's completely normal. No matter how successful we are and no matter how far we go in our businesses, everyone falls back to level 1 consciousness; that's just part of the human experience. At this point, I want to highlight that level 1 and level 2 are where we forget who we truly are, and many people live in this forgotten state almost their entire lives.

Personally, I don't think of the first two levels as being "bad" or "wrong." To me, they're secret portals that lead to the highest levels of consciousness, and I don't want you to feel like you've made some kind of mistake when you inevitably fall back to these lower levels. *Everyone* experiences falling back, and the most empowering thing to do is to recognize what's going on. When we're aware of it—when we recognize what it feels like to be on the lower levels of consciousness—we can purposefully step through the secret portal and quickly move up into higher levels of consciousness and instantly remember the truth of our own limitless capacity to create what we desire.

Level 2 Consciousness: Fight

Level 2 consciousness is fueled by a powerful limiting belief: "success takes hard work." The thing about limiting beliefs is that they become self-fulfilling prophecies. If you believe success takes hard work, you'll create circumstances in your business to make yourself right, and this perpetuates the need to "fight to win." At level 2, the drive to succeed is so intense that you'll feel like you're about to collapse under the pressure at any second. As a result, your primary feelings are anger, frustration, irritation, resistance, defiance, antagonism, and struggle.

At level 2, *efforting* is the name of the game. It's all about the effort and the hard work. You hustle, and you push, and everything feels like an uphill battle. Level 2 is where you strive and burn the candle at both ends, and this is the level where everyday entrepreneurs turn into workaholics who can't seem to remember how to shut down their computers. Ultimately, this is where most people burn out, and it looks like you're driving full speed ahead, but from an energetic viewpoint, you're driving full speed *with the brakes on*.

The biggest problem with level 2 consciousness is that it creates what I like to call a "mirage of achievement." It feels like you've achieved real success, but the truth is you're deeply unhappy. Success at level 2 is about sacrifice, and you give up a lot of what's close to your heart—like spending time with the ones you love the most—just to get what you want in your business. You don't see any other way to accomplish your goals, and you drive yourself into the ground in an effort to do it all. You keep telling yourself that things will be different when you get to your goals, but nothing changes.

Meanwhile, money continuously flows into your business, you have a waitlist of clients, or maybe you have an endless line of customers who can't seem to get enough of your products or services. You might even be the envy of other entrepreneurs because everything's going so well, but people don't know that you're hiding a dirty little secret. You get zero joy and satisfaction from your work—and you have no time to enjoy the successes you create.

Shifting Up from Level 2

At level 2, everything you experience confirms and reinforces the belief that you must work hard and sacrifice what you love to see success in your business. This is a result of black-and-white thinking, and it's a serious problem because it triggers toxic judgment. Everyone and everything is right or wrong or positive or negative, which stops you from moving forward because there isn't any wiggle room for creativity, expansion, or innovation.

Shifting out of level 2 is about recognizing where you're closing your mind off, where you're so certain that you've hit on the right way, and that your way is the best way and there's no other way to create what you want in your business that could be better than the path that you've already identified. It's about opening your mind and looking at what's going on in your business through a new lens that may actually support in expanding, moving forward, and achieving success without sacrifice.

The other element of level 2 to watch for is a feeling of self-doubt, which shows up as the inability to fully trust yourself in your decisions. You don't trust that you'll be able to handle growth or an influx of clients—or that you'll really deliver results and keep your promises.

A powerful way to cultivate trust is to go deep within and start to follow your feelings. Where do you feel passion? Where do you feel excited? What inspires you? What feels like fun in your business? What feels like flow? Taking massive action on these positive-feeling areas and opportunities can create massive momentum and get you results much more quickly and easily.

Level 3 Consciousness: Cope

At level 3, you're moving out of struggle, survival, and sacrifice and into focused positive energy and self-mastery. Fears and worries from the previous two levels begin to dissolve, and entrepreneurs at level 3 are starting to move into a positive, productive space. Level 3 consciousness is the place where "lemons turn into lemonade" because the primary experience here is finding ways to cope with obstacles and challenges so you can make the best of things.

Level 3 is the first level of consciousness where you're attracting and creating from a powerful, intentional place. This is the level where the energy of expansion overrides the restrictive, fearful energy of defensive protection. This is where you start to build your business in a way that supports your growth and potential versus doing whatever it takes to escape failure in your business even if some of these experiences ultimately trigger growth and wisdom. That said, when you're at level 3, you're still a long way off from hitting your full potential. This level basically works like a Band-Aid that temporarily fixes the challenges of levels 1 and 2, and while you're starting to release a lot of the fears, worries, anxiety, frustrations, and anger that you were using to drive your business forward in the previous levels, you're not totally free from it.

One of the superpowers of level 3 consciousness is that you know how to rationalize and cope with challenges and obstacles. You can explain away the things that aren't working well for you in your business, and you can talk yourself—and often others—into thinking and feeling like everything's okay.

But the reality is you're still experiencing a lot of the negativity, struggles, and primary emotions of levels 1 and 2. At level 3, you're *really* good at making yourself feel better so you can continue making progress. This is much better place to be in than the other two levels, but you're nowhere near your most powerful point of consciousness.

The most attractive element about level 3 is also the most dangerous. Knowing how to cope creates a feeling of safety and comfort, but it also keeps you stuck. Way too many entrepreneurs never rise above level 3 consciousness because they're afraid to rock the boat, push the boundaries, take risks in the business, jump off the edge, and fly.

Shifting Up from Level 3

Getting out of level 3 can be tricky. There is very little motivation or inspiration to shift out of this level because being at level 3 feels safe and secure. So, if you're serious about rising to higher levels of consciousness, you need to work with the *slingshot effect*. This is about letting yourself slide back a little bit into level 2 consciousness so you can tap into some of the "fight" to drive yourself upward. Letting yourself be driven to win will give you the energy and focus you need to rise out of the comfort and routine of level 3. One of the most effective ways to borrow some "fight" from level 2 is to unhook from the feeling of "good enough" that characterizes level 3.

At level 3, we tend to invest a lot of energy in keeping the "difficult" or "challenging" parts of our business—and our own shortcomings as entrepreneurs—hidden from our conscious minds. It's where we keep these "shadows" locked in our unconscious minds, and this holds us back from truly stepping into our boldest vision and purpose as metaconscious entrepreneurs. Basically, at level 3, your business is doing well and you're achieving a lot of your goals, but you're nowhere near your potential—and a deeper part of you *knows* it.

What you need to do is unhook from "good enough" and embrace your whole self, including the shadows, so you can have full access to all of your energy and tap into the *fight* from level 2. A great way to kick-start this process is to start asking yourself questions that can help unearth the stuff that's hidden in your unconscious, the things that are draining your energy and blocking your full potential.

I've found that these 6 powerful *shadow questions* can get the job done, and there's only one rule: focus on being brutally honest with yourself because what we want is to get to the truth no matter how awkward or uncomfortable it may be in the moment. I encourage you to write your answers in a physical journal (not on your computer). The act of writing can help you tap into your unconscious to release hidden thoughts, beliefs, and truths. Ready? Here we go:

- Shadow Question 1: What am I tolerating?
- Shadow Question 2: Where am I settling?
- Shadow Question 3: Where are things good enough—but there's potential for so much better?
- Shadow Question 4: What would going all in look like?
- Shadow Question 5: What would feel scary and exciting at the same time?

Stacy Hartmann

- Shadow Question 6: How can I push the envelope here?

Level 4 Consciousness: Love

This is the level of pure love, and it's where you begin to transform into a metaconscious entrepreneur. Level 4 is the rich soil in which high vibrational, world-changing conscious businesses start to grow and thrive. Level 4 is the door that opens into the field of infinite creation. Level 4 is where instant manifestations happen—and all possibilities exist. At level 4, you're starting to become recognized and accepted as the authority or expert in your field or industry. When your consciousness is consistently vibrating at level 4, you'll quickly create a thriving, lucrative, wealth-generating business that's also creating a positive impact on the world.

The biggest difference between level 4 consciousness and the first three levels is that you're all about serving others and creating powerful, meaningful, nurturing relationships. The other three levels are all about asking, "What's in it for me, myself, and I?"

Level 4 is the first level that takes you out of focusing on yourself, your goals, and your dreams. You're about contributing to the world as you step into deep service that can create lasting transformations for your clients, your customers, your team, and everyone else. Level 4 is where running a business is a spiritual activity. It's where the need to be first, to be right, to always be ahead, to compete, and to be better—the needs and desires of the human ego—begin to disappear.

At this level, you start to see that making decisions from the ego, evaluating partnerships and opportunities, expanding, and growing the business from a place of ego is ultimately damaging to your business, and it will hold you back from rising to your highest potential. Where there is ego, there is fear and doubt, and where there is fear and doubt, there is restriction, constriction, and destruction.

Metaconscious Entrepreneur

But when you're at the level 4 consciousness, and when you're vibrating at the frequency of love, the focus is on building real relationships with every single person who touches your business: leads, prospects, clients, customers, team members, and service providers. The power of level 4 consciousness arises from nurturing these relationships, expressing real love, and then receiving love in return. Make no mistake ... this is powerful stuff!

Most entrepreneurs feel alone in what they want to do and how they want to make a difference in the world. They crave deep connections and a feeling of true belonging, and to really receive these beautiful, bountiful energies, we must be willing to give generously from our hearts. When we give from our hearts and give with love without expecting *anything* in return, we create raving fans and massive loyalty without even trying. This is where you get to let go of the hustle, the pushing, and the "efforting" that mark the previous levels of consciousness. This is where you step into the energy of easeful manifestation, expansion, and positivity.

The reason? Everyone who comes across you and your business—people who work with you, people who buy from you, and people who experience what you do—cannot wait to shout from the rooftops! They want to spread the word, they want to help you, and they want to share what you do with their friends and their families. They want to refer people to you again and again, and this creates massive sustainability. It makes marketing—and sales—a total breeze. Customers and clients who connect with you through referrals and through word of mouth are already ready to say yes to you because they trust the person who referred you to them—and they trust you.

I've had direct experience with level 4 consciousness and what it can do for business. A few years ago, I had the opportunity to be a lead trainer for weekend retreats and seminars for one of the top coach training and personal development companies in the world. It didn't pay a lot, and it meant missing weekends with my family, but I felt drawn to doing the work. Every time we organized an event, I had a chance to interact with students, train them, and teach them how to become the most powerful coaches on the planet. I was constantly giving information, sharing information, and supporting them in becoming the best and owning their craft without any expectations.

As a result, I built real relationships with my ideal audience, and the connections I made at the time run so deep that it led to a multiple six-figure business in record time (and my business is still growing!) Just showing up and training and teaching without any offers—or any idea that it might generate business—opens the gate wide and lets you stand out from the crowd and create the impact that you want to create in the world. Trust me ... the money, prestige, customers, and endless waitlist of clients will follow.

Shifting Up from Level 4

The good thing about level 4 consciousness is that it feels so aligned and so good to be loved and to give to your clients and customers freely with love, but here's the paradox: all of that good stuff can work *against* you.

Let's face it—it feels good to be loved and to give love, and it's tempting to stay where you are and never shift up from this level, but the truth is building a successful business and reaching into the heights of what you can do in the field of infinite creation isn't about stagnation. It's about growing and expanding past your comfort zone and into levels 5, 6, and 7. So, it's important to stay excited, motivated, and inspired about building an ultra-successful business.

The secret to staying in the energy of excitement has to do with getting crystal clear about how you want to serve in your business and what and how you want to serve your clients and customers. Start creating a plan about what you want to teach, share, and offer and how do you want to deliver your expertise.

Then step into that space of expertise so you can confidently start showing up in communities both online and offline, including social media, weekend seminars, and conferences.

Shifting up from level 4 is about stretching yourself and walking through the fear of being authentic and vulnerable, owning your whole story and the impact that it can have on inspiring other people, moving other people, and helping other people.

So, commit to showing up authentically and vulnerably in everything you're doing in your marketing and in your sales. Give yourself permission to finally get creative and show up in your unique, authentic way.

Level 5 Consciousness: Inspire

When you get to level 5 consciousness, you're at what I like to call the entrepreneur's sweet spot because you're still totally grounded in your human experience, but you can manifest phenomenal results in your business. You're at the point where you can really expand your potential in ways that get you massive results, and you'll rise up to high levels of influence and authority. The core energy and experience around level 5 consciousness is *we all win—or we don't play.*

Some of the most successful entrepreneurs in the world—people like Steve Jobs and Richard Branson—operate at level 5. They're in an entire new space of self-mastery, and they're so powerful and confident that their energy is contagious. They have complete faith that no matter what their choices and decisions in business, it's going to turn out for the best.

When you're at level 5, you have the skill of seeing things as they are, and you can release judgment. You no longer see everything around you and what's going on in your business as good or bad or black and white. You know that things are what they are; it's just what it is.

This nonjudgmental approach keeps you from spiraling down into self-blame and thinking, *I should have known better* or *That didn't work, and it was my fault.* Instead, you're calm and centered no matter what happens. This gives you the emotional and mental space you need to stay open to every opportunity that comes your way. At level 5, you know there's no such thing as failure because you understand that you're here to learn and that everything is a lesson and an experiment in your business. You're ready to take fast action so you can tweak, adjust, pivot, and keep moving forward. Level 5 consciousness feels magical because it lets you get more done in a fraction of the time it takes others to accomplish the same tasks. This is because you're no longer experiencing "energy leaks" through self-judgment, criticism, and self-blame.

Shifting Up from Level 5

There are a lot of decisions to make at level 5 because you're attracting and magnetizing incredible opportunities in your business. Maybe you'll be invited to speak at high-profile conventions or seminars. You might be asked to teach or partner with influencers and world-class organizations that will skyrocket your visibility, grow your audience, and establish your authority in your field. It'll feel like most of these opportunities come to you out of nowhere, and because you're pretty much "drowning" in these juicy opportunities, you'll find yourself getting lost in the fear of missing out (FOMO).

So, the key to shifting up from level 5 into levels 6 and 7 is to train yourself in the art of focused discernment. Basically, it's about learning to say no so you can say yes *only* to opportunities that are truly aligned with your business. A big part of cultivating laser-sharp focus and discernment is recognizing that your power of choice expands beyond the opportunities that come your way.

Shifting out of level 5 is about cultivating self-trust and knowing that letting go of some opportunities so you can be in full alignment with your mission—and this means letting go and saying no more often—allows you to tap into your ability to manifest without limits as you continue to take fast action in line with your biggest boldest dreams and goals for your business.

Level 6 Consciousness: Create

At the lower levels of consciousness—particularly levels 1 through 3—it's all about the ego. We see ourselves as clearly separate from everybody else and very separate from GUS. In the next 2 levels of consciousness—levels 4 and 5—the ego is diminished, but it is a significant presence. There is a strong sense of self versus others. At level 6 and 7, there is no ego, and it's completely transcended, which is why level 6 is considered the level of self-transcendence.

This is where you start to see that you are a part of something bigger—much bigger—than what can be seen or touched. This is where you begin sensing and experiencing the world of energy. Level 6 consciousness takes you deep into a magical sense of oneness with all things. You begin to realize that you are connected to everyone and everything—everywhere—and we are all part of an incredible unseen tapestry of energy that stretches through time and throughout existence. Self-transcendence is a reward in and of itself as this feeling of oneness brings with it a sense of belonging, love, joy, peace, and freedom unlike anything else you might have experienced.

At level 6, you are connecting and creating from a deeper spiritual vibration and from the very core of your being. You are in touch with your full power and the expansiveness and unlimitedness of who you are. Level 6 energy is incredibly potent, and it can bring your wildest dreams and desires into your reality for the highest good of all. However, it's important to know that level 6 is unsustainable in the day-to-day running of your business.

Level 6 consciousness is about always remaining deep in spiritual awareness, and as a result, you experience flow. Flow is a state where you experience unwavering presence and complete energetic engagement in a task that causes you to lose track of time and be immersed in an activity that feels joyful—even if it's mundane. This gives you the power to impact the world from an energetic and consciousness standpoint, but it takes you out of your human experience. So, when it comes to creating a conscious business, the high vibrational frequencies of levels 6 and 7 are for tapping into—rather than for full, sustained—immersion.

So, what you need to know here is that at level 6, we have access to 90 percent of the potential available to us. When you hit level 6, your productivity and performance go through the roof because you know everything, and everyone is a part of you just like you are a part of everything and everyone. This creates an energetic space that is free of judgment, blame, and criticism; you no longer have any of these low-vibrational energies blocking your innate power and potential. If everyone is a part of you, there's nothing left to judge!

The primary experience at level 6 is pure joy, brilliant creativity, and courage. You can step into flow and lose track of time and space as you allow creative energy to move through you and out into the world in your marketing, in your offers, and in your services.

Level 6 is also all about opportunity, and there's no good or bad. There's nothing to "improve" because it's the *experience* that counts.

You'll know you're at level 6 when you start to live from your intuition—that higher wisdom, that information, that gut instinct that comes through—and when that information comes through, you have one job, which is to step back down into the fifth level of consciousness and take fast, massive action. You can maximize the power of level 6 when you're willing to take risks and have deep trust in GUS and your intuition.

At level 6, you understand that there's higher guidance governing everything and everyone. You receive amazing creative insights all the time, out of nowhere. This is where creativity comes alive, and when these creative ideas and inspirations come from a place that is higher than ourselves, their success and impact on the world are inevitable.

The essence of being at level 6 is pure presence. So, when you're connecting with people in your business, when you're connecting with partners, and when you're connecting with anyone in any relationship, you can facilitate deep synchronicity and serendipity and being on the same wavelength by using intuitive listening. You're completely connected and extremely engaged in the present moment. You're able to start picking up on and hearing the things that aren't being said out loud. This is an incredibly powerful skill to have in sales and in marketing—across the board. So, tapping into level 6 consciousness leads to a feeling of being unstoppable, a feeling of immense power, and a deep soul connection.

Shifting Up from Level 6

At level 6, you can connect with your soul tribe in business. Everyone you meet, work with, and serve feels deeply understood, seen, valued, and loved in a way that they probably have never been before.

Shifting up to the level 7—the highest level of consciousness—is about connecting with the truth that we are all one. It's about opening and allowing creative energy to come through you as you continue to trust and release judgment of yourself and others so you can step into flow and tap into your intuition to make decisions in your business.

At level 6, your consciousness turns to the spiritual, and having a regular meditation practice, staying mindful as you cultivate present moment awareness while adopting other spiritual intuitive and reflective practices such as journaling, and connecting with a like-minded group of conscious spiritual entrepreneurs will open the door to the next and highest level of consciousness.

Level 7 Consciousness: Manifest

At level 7, you finally achieve 100 percent of your potential. This is where you live from the true essence of who you are as you release all the blocks and the lower levels of consciousness. Level 7 is a place of nonjudgment, objective thinking, fearlessness, and absolute passion. There is no such thing as hierarchy at this level, and nothing and no one is better or worse than anything or anyone else. At level 7, you are as passionate about a leaf on a tree as you are about your purpose and mission and what you want to share with the world.

Level 7 is all about creation, which means that you can manifest, observe, and participate at the same time—and you can see and experience all levels of consciousness as you work with each level in whatever way you choose. At level 7, winning and losing are illusions. In fact, everything is an illusion: time is an illusion, money is an illusion, and we are an illusion. Entrepreneurs who know how to tap into level 7 consciousness are the most powerful people in the world.

Level 4 is the level of love and of selfless service, but level 7 is the energy of unconditional love. Level 7 is deeply spiritual. This is the level where you are the observer and the participant at the same time. The primary experience here is unconditional love, fearlessness, absolute passion, and complete nonjudgment. No one can completely resonate and sustain this level of consciousness except for masters such as Jesus Christ and the Buddha; therefore, some people think of level 7 energy as *Christ consciousness* or *Buddha consciousness*.

At level 7, you're experiencing the wholeness of the universe in that moment. You're so completely tapped in the moment that you might find it preferable to be alone. If you're vibrating level 7 consciousness, you could appear aloof, uncaring, and disconnected to the outside world, but you're unconditionally loving and accepting of every single soul and every single person on the planet—no matter their values or beliefs.

Level 7 consciousness is as powerful as it is rare, but when you do get to tap into you, you can do anything. The field of infinite creation is your playground, and instant manifestations are effortless.

Expanding into Level 7

At level 7, your mind—with all of its fears and doubts—is no longer running the show. You are fully connected to your heart and your intuition, and when you get inspired, creative ideas and insights, you don't wait. You take action right away.

Just like level 6, expanding into level 7 happens through meditation, prayer, and quieting the mind. So, whatever it takes to step into a tranquil, peaceful inner state will have a huge impact in helping you open up into level 7 consciousness. The more you spend time in a meditative state, the more you get to dig in to that delicious, infinitely potent level 7 energy because GUS gets to communicate with you when the mind is free of unnecessary thoughts, ruminations, and chatter.

This definitely is *not* easy to do, but it's absolutely worth it because magic and miracles can happen in an instant when you tap in to level 7 consciousness. I know because it happened to me when I was working with at-risk youth. Even now, I can hardly believe what happened. It was wildly synchronistic and super powerful, and everything I wanted and needed unfolded with perfect grace and alignment because I let myself trust in my intuition and in the phenomenal power of level 7 consciousness.

At the time, the organization I was with had put together a phenomenal program. We knew it would be transformational for the kids because they'd get the chance to gain some real-world work experience. The idea was to create a social enterprise out of the program we had created, which would fund itself, and we could scale it and reach even more young people who needed it. We knew there was a fierce competition for grants. I came up with this idea that if we could create a win-win-win situation. The students received work experience while doing the work, which would then generate revenue to fund the program. I had the basic idea, but I didn't know what to do with it or how it would work. I let it brew and percolate in the back of my mind. I did what I knew I had to do: I believed that we would get everything we needed, and then I let it go. I stopped thinking about the "how."

A few days later, I received a strong urge to go to a restaurant my grandma used to own before she passed away. The new owner had turned it into an ice-cream shop, and I was suddenly drawn to going there. I was *not* in the mood for ice cream. I wasn't hungry for ice cream, but the ice cream there is really good! I just knew I had to go there.

At first, I thought it had something to do with my grandma. I was curious, and I knew enough about energy to know that you don't argue with GUS! I drove to the shop and walked in. The owner happened to be there. He introduced himself, and I liked him right away. He was down-to-earth, friendly, and incredibly genuine and authentic.

After chatting for a few minutes, I said, "My grandma used to own this shop before she died."

He immediately said he was sorry to hear about my grandma's passing, and we started talking about our families and our lives. Somewhere in the middle of the deep conversation, he shared his philosophy about business and how he loves to hire students who nobody else will hire. His mission was to train them and teach them the power of work ethic and the impact that it has on businesses.

It felt like a light was suddenly flooding in my heart and mind. I instantly understood that this was the person we were looking for to help with the program! He was going to be the one who would help the kids we were working with—and that's exactly what happened. We created a strategic partnership and innovated an entire social enterprise that started with that "chance" meeting at the ice-cream shop that used to be my grandma's restaurant.

It was the ultimate serendipitous, synchronistic experience. This man had all the business acumen and all the knowledge—everything we didn't have. We had kids who wanted work experience, and we had the people to implement all of it. It was a match made in heaven! It was amazing to give these kids the opportunity to really experience work and step into entrepreneurship. They did phenomenally well in that program, and they were the ones who nobody thought would even graduate from high school!

So, that's an example of the synchronistic, serendipitous flow that comes from being in level 7 consciousness. Just being in that place of trust opens up so many doors, and this higher guidance is there for you every step of the way. And that is when you know you are on purpose in your consciousness and truly tapping into massive amounts of energy that create the legacy and love you want to create in your business as a metaconscious entrepreneur while also generating the wealth you want for the life that you dream of.

PART II

THE TRUTH ABOUT CONSCIOUS SUCCESS AND ABUNDANCE

CHAPTER 9

The Awareness Code

Our greatest potential is already within us, and this means we have what it takes to create and to manifest anything and everything we want. However, we've been conditioned to search for answers *outside* ourselves. We've been conditioned to deny what we feel in the moment.

Armchair psychologists and the mainstream media tell us to "think positive" and "stay optimistic" no matter what. (Even if you've only ever read *one* mainstream self-help book, you know what I'm talking about!) There is no need to try to be positive because you were born with full access to the highest levels of positive, creative energy.

When you entered the world, you were literally living inside the field of infinite creation. You did not experience separation from your mother or father, and you did not experience separation from anything or anyone. You were pure love, and you were one with all of creation. We can feel this beautiful, powerful energy when we are around babies. It's that feeling you get when you hold a newborn in your arms—there's this sense of wonder, connection, and deep serenity. When my sons were babies, I could hold them for hours and hours. I would feel peace wash over me, and when we were together, the world fell away. Nothing else mattered. Time dissolved, and I didn't know if seconds, minutes, or hours had gone by. I became lost in just *being* with them. I was connected to the highest levels of energy and consciousness while holding my baby boys in my arms, and my worries and cares melted away. I was simply being present to pure, unconditional love.

This incredible, almost otherworldly experience is essentially an energetic phenomenon called *entrainment*. Entrainment works just like a mirror except that it does a lot more than reflect what's on the surface. When we hold a baby, our energy literally entrains to the baby's high vibrational positive energy, and we can easily be present and in the moment with them.

As we grow into adulthood, it can feel like we're disconnected, and we've lost this beautiful high vibrational positive energy—this oneness—with all of creation. We believe we can no longer radiate and vibrate at the highest levels of consciousness, but that's not the case. We *never* lose this inborn ability, and the secret to bringing it back to our consciousness is to let go of everything that is *not* us. It's about coming home to ourselves, and it means we must stop being anything other than who we truly are. Otherwise, we end up blocking our capacity to create and manifest what we desire. So, instead of aiming to be a "better, more positive" person, the real magic happens when you focus on dissolving the veil that is covering the truth of who we are. That is what *the awareness code* is about.

The awareness code is essentially about releasing three key elements—attachment, judgment, and fear—which I like to call *energy collapsers*. The three collapsers work like a dense fog that prevents you from being who you are and from seeing anything other than that which is directly in front of you. It gives you tunnel vision, gets you to continuously chase your tail, and leaves you feeling like you're being pulled in multiple directions. You never get the chance to return to your true nature of oneness and pure love. It holds you back from envisioning a bigger life and going for a bigger dream. Instead, you get stuck in the mud and continue to play small in your business and in your life.

Something amazing happens when you discover the truth of the awareness code and the three energy collapsers. Knowing how these collapsers work empowers you to release the fear, judgment, and attachment that keep you from achieving your limitless potential. It lets you rise to higher and higher levels of consciousness with ease, and as you deepen your awareness and let go of each of the three collapsers, you can quickly unlock remarkable creativity, which leads to beautiful, bold, bright business visions, ideas, and insights. These diamonds are hiding in plain sight.

As you continue to release the collapsers, you will cultivate self-trust so you can consistently take action with faith in your abilities and the courage to take the actions you need to take to grow your business to greater and greater heights of service and abundance. Through the rest of this chapter, we'll take a close look at each of the three energy collapsers so we can shine the light of awareness and start to release each one.

Energy Collapser 1: Attachment

Attachment is any action, thought, or emotion where your sole purpose is to get something or go somewhere other than where you are. Attachment instantly pulls you out of your immediate, direct experience and into a desired future outcome. As a result, it keeps you from experiencing happiness, fulfillment, peace, and other high-vibrating energies right here, right now.

Attachment invites low-vibrational feelings and emotions like disappointment, impatience, craving, not enough-ness, striving, hustling, and a belief that you can't ever be whole and complete unless the outcome you're looking for becomes your reality. Ultimately, attachment sets you up for victimhood, and it steals your creative power. It brings you down to the lowest levels of energy and consciousness because you're consistently putting your passions and happiness on hold as you hold our breath and wait for something that may or may not happen in the future. This is a major block when it comes to connecting to GUS and the field of infinite creation where instant manifestations happen.

The secret to releasing attachment is to accept your reality *as it is*, to embrace *where* you are and *who* you are, and to fall in love with the *process* and the journey of achieving your desire or goal. Doing this lets you to rise in your power and your energy as you move forward—from moment to moment—with love, curiosity, excitement, enthusiasm, creativity, and beautiful, high-vibrational energies that consistently keep you playing in the field of infinite creation.

Energy Collapser 2: Fear

- The Fear of Rejection
- The Fear of Failure
- The Fear of Success
- The Fear of Loss
- The Fear of Power

Fear is a decoy that steals your true power and purpose on this planet, which is why it's crucial that you understand and activate a deep, spiritual truth: Being fearless does not mean you don't feel fear. Being fearless means you are no longer afraid of fear. Being fearless means you can feel fear, acknowledge fear, and do what you need to do in this moment and the next moment and the next. It means you can take aligned action that will move you toward your desires, your purpose, and your passion and use the energy of fear to achieve breathtaking breakthroughs in your mental, spiritual, and emotional evolution. These breakthroughs will allow you to rise up and serve as a fully conscious, wildly successful, and abundant entrepreneur.

One of fastest ways to acknowledge fear and release the "fear of fear itself" is with something I call the *fear annihilator process*. It's a powerful yet simple five-step technique, and here's how it works:

Step 1: The Warrior Way

First, face your fears like a warrior. In other words, face your fears head-on! The first thing to do is to work through the sentence prompts below. They're designed to help you bring hidden fears up into the light. Keep in mind that all your fears and limiting beliefs come from your past experiences, and when you let your inner fears have a voice or give your fears a chance to be heard, something magical happens: they start to lose their power!

You're probably feeling some resistance against working through these sentence prompts. If this happens, I invite you to take a deep breath, let it out, and set the intention to trust the process. Remember that our fears exist whether we acknowledge them or not, and we can only be free of our fears when we acknowledge them. So, go ahead, dive in, and be brutally honest!

- The biggest reason I won't step up to fulfill my boldest business dream, goal, and vision is because _____.
- I will never get what I want in my business because _____.
- I'm not ready to play big in my business because _____.
- It's not safe for me to unleash my gifts, skills, and talents into the world because _____.
- I'm not doing what it really takes to expand my wealth and impact because _____.
- I believe I'm not worthy of being seen as a revolutionary leader because _____.
- I just can't _____ because _____.
- This is what I'm telling myself about <insert a challenge or obstacle that you're currently facing> _____.

I know this exercise isn't exactly fun, but it's definitely worth working through all of them. When you let your fears have a voice, you'll start to let them go even if they've been around for decades (check out steps 2–5 for more on this).

Step 2: Get Real

Now that you've brought your fears and limiting beliefs up into the light, it's time to test their validity. Ask yourself this powerful question with relation to everything you uncovered in step 1.

- Is this fear real and true for me? (Yes or No)

Don't overthink it. Just answer the question without wondering why it is or isn't real and true. Anytime you move beyond a simple yes-or-no answer, you're getting into justification, and that strengthens the fear.

Step 3: Acknowledge and Annihilate

Now you're ready to get to the truth *behind* your fears. This game-changing question will get you there:

- Do I have a valid reason to *not* go for my soul purpose and my biggest business goals—the things I know I was put on this earth to do?

If your answer is a strong yes, it means you have yet to tap into the depth of your biggest purpose: your soul purpose. You'll need to rework, refine, or reimagine your soul purpose and then go back to step 1.

Step 4: Say It Like You Mean It

Steps 1 through 3 are the hardest part of the fear annihilator process. Once you've worked through those steps, you'll see that your fears are absolutely not valid—and then you're ready to fully commit your energy and consciousness to your biggest, boldest business vision and mission. I want you to say this mantra out loud:

- I am committed to building a conscious business, being wildly wealthy, and creating the impact I was born to create in the world.

Keep saying this at least three times a day, every day, until it feels like you've fully and unequivocally embodied your commitment to your goals.

Step 5: JFDI (Just F'ing Do It!)

Your final step has to do with bringing your dreams, visions, and goals from the realm of thought, energy, and consciousness into the realm of grounded, tangible reality. You can do this when you take rapid, massive, aligned action. Action brings clarity and anchors your new mantra from step 4 deep into your energy and consciousness.

Go ahead and list out all the actions, ideas, and insights that are coming through for you right now. Write them down in your journal or on your device or computer. Since this is a *living* list, keep adding to it whenever a new idea pops into your mind. Remember that action is where it's at! The greater the gap between insight and action, the greater the likelihood the three energy collapsers—especially fear—will enter your heart and mind and stop you from moving forward.

Energy Collapser 3: Judgment

Judgment is *anything* that we view through the lens of "better than" or "hierarchy." It's probably the most destructive of the three energy collapsers because GUS is the energy that creates worlds. This energy freely flows through the field of infinite creation. Since it is pure love, it knows no judgment.

When we judge and pick apart everything and everyone we encounter, we're unhooking from GUS and cutting ourselves off from the field of infinite creation. We end up inadvertently blocking our ability to manifest and cocreate our desires.

If you want to stay connected to the field of infinite creation where instant manifestations happen, if you want to consistently receive groundbreaking, game-changing creative input directly from GUS—the kind of input that can explode your impact and your income in your business—then you must know how to recognize and drop judgment.

Here are the two key judgment types that hold you back from becoming a master manifester in your business.

Type 1: Self-Judgment

Millions of people have become obsessed with personal growth. Their intentions are good, but they miss the core negative belief in a lot of self-help books and courses:

- You are flawed and need to "fix" yourself in order to tap into your fullest potential.

But here's the thing:

- You are *not* flawed. None of us are.
- You are perfectly imperfect, and you can skip all the "fixing" and go straight into accepting the truth.
- You are all things.
- You are a limitless spiritual being—*and* you are human.
- You are selfish—*and* generous.
- You are loving—*and* unloving.
- You are unlimited—*and* limited.
- You are all things.

So, rather than trying to *not* be something, accept *all* of who you are. In this acceptance, you can rise up, release all self-judgment, and align with GUS—the energy that creates worlds—to create and design your world exactly as you want it to be.

Type 2: Problem Versus Possibility

Way too many conscious, world-changing entrepreneurs unconsciously hold themselves back from hitting their goals and making their dreams a reality because they believe business is a game called "Figuring Things Out." They believe that once everything's figured out, they're good to go—and they never have to worry or think about their problems again. They believe that once they figure out how to get clients, reach a bigger audience, build a great product, or create massive wealth, they'll never have to worry about any of that again.

It's a collective human belief that when we get through the crap and solve the "problem," we're done! However, the opposite is true. If you are judging something or someone as a problem to solve, you're creating space for more problems to come to you.

And when you're focused on problems, you can't see possibility.

A lot of people think solving problems creates possibility, but that's one of the biggest "personal growth" lies around. The truth is possibility already exists, and it's *definitely* not hiding inside a problem! So, release the judgment. Stop judging what's going on as a problem and switch into looking for a possibility instead.

Pursuing the problem to get to the possibility is like going to the back door of your house to get to the front door. Getting straight to the possibility is your shortcut, and it boils down to your ability to drop judgment and choose where you want to invest your energy: problem or possibility? While this seems like an easy choice, what does it take to live in the choice of possibility? An unshakeable inner knowing that infinite possibility always exists.

Stacy Hartmann

    You need this knowing deep in your bones—like every cell of your body is chanting, "Possibility!" Everything you are seeing and interpreting actually has nothing to do with what actually *is*. You'll come to realize that when you live in possibility, you're living in the field of infinite creation where your desires can become your reality *just like that!*

CHAPTER 10

The Alignment Code

As we've discovered so far in this book, beneath the visible and the tangible, there's an incredibly powerful web of unseen energy that governs all things, which is the field of infinite creation. I know the field exists with every ounce of my being because I've seen the magic—and miracles—that can happen in business and in life when we tap into it.

When I learned to master the inner workings of the field by being in alignment with the seven precepts from part I and working with the seven levels of consciousness, I created $100,000 in my business in ninety days. It happened with an idea that came to me out of nowhere, and I went ahead and doubled that $100,000 a few months later! I didn't *earn* that revenue in the way most entrepreneurs do. I didn't push, and I didn't hustle. I didn't get on countless sales calls with potential clients. I didn't share or promote my offer on Facebook five times a day, every day—plus weekends—and I definitely didn't build out a massive, complicated sales funnel.

Every last dime of that $100,000 came to me without a single public offer. I tuned into my energy, and I dialed up to the frequency and the level of consciousness that I wanted to call in: levels 5, 6 and 7. I stepped into deep trust, knowing that GUS would bring me wealth-generating, world-changing ideas, creativity, and wisdom—and that's exactly what happened. This might seem strange or even unbelievable, but extraordinary things happen all the time when you learn to work with your energy. Effort is removed from the equation, and everything in your business begins to flow.

All this magic unfolds when you practice being deeply aware of where your personal energy is at any moment and then work with your energy to alchemize what's standing in your way as you become aligned with everything you want to create in your business—that's what the alignment code does. It transforms you into the most potent, magical, magnetic, fiery version of you so you can take charge of everything that's happening in your space and start creating out-of-this-world results in your business.

In the awareness code, you learned about the three energy collapsers (attachment, fear, and judgment) that hold you back from rising to higher levels of consciousness and potential. Now you're going to learn to transform and alchemize those collapsers with the four quantum powers of the *alignment code.*

The Power of Giving

The legendary psychoanalyst Sigmund Freud believed there is no such thing as altruism because, at some level, we're all thinking, "What's in it for me?" This is usually the case in entrepreneurship, but when you can approach your business and give from a place of no expectations and no strings attached, something remarkable happens. You achieve a powerful inner state that I like to call *detached involvement,* and it's where you're crystal clear on your goals and clear in your vision for your business, but you are not attached to having it happen exactly the way you want it to. This is one of the fastest ways to move up the consciousness scale to levels 5, 6, and 7, which is where you become aligned with the energy of the field of infinite creation. So, when you're ready to harness the power of giving with detached involvement, I want you to ask yourself. "What can I give to another with zero expectations?"

There was a point where I was working with this question and answering this question in my business every single day. I kept asking, "What can I give to another with zero expectations?

Metaconscious Entrepreneur

What can I share or teach that would get people real results and breakthroughs? What if I gave it all away for free?"

I never failed to receive an answer (often more than one), and the answer always came to me in an intuitive hit. Sometimes I got a message to share a free teaching on social media or to offer a free session as a gift. No matter what I received, I "showed the eff up" to deliver, deliver, deliver! As I mentioned at the start of this chapter, I created $100,000 in ninety days without making a single public offer because my creativity and abundance of information and inspiration shot through the roof—and everything flowed in my business with ease.

So much mind-blowing stuff happens with the *power of giving* because when you work with this segment of the alignment code, you unlock two transformational processes or effects:

- the multiplier effect
- the boomerang effect

Both are interconnected—you can't have one without the other—and here's how they work ...

When all you're doing is focusing on yourself, you limit the amount of energy that can flow through to you because there is only *one* of you, but when you expand out and focus on more people, you're multiplying the output. And because everything is energy and energy creates, it only makes sense that the more energy you give to others, the faster you receive the energy to create even more. In this way, you get to rapidly multiply your output to ten times, a hundred times, or a thousand times in your business. This is the multiplier effect in action, and it triggers the boomerang effect.

Think of the boomerang effect as an energetic reward system where you'll always receive what you give—and more! When the boomerang effect gets going, everything that comes from you returns to you. When you keep tapping in to the *power of giving*, everything you desire will be fully materialized and manifested, including your wildest business goals and dreams. The power of giving is an incredible way to get what you want and more while being of service and showing up as who you truly are: limitless, unconditional love and potential.

The Power of Connection

When I first started working with many of my clients, I noticed that they were consumed with planning, making lists, and creating strategies and offers in their business. There's nothing wrong with that, and it's important, but it's also critical to remember that anything you do behind the scenes in your business—anything that keeps you hidden behind your computer—also keeps you disconnected from people. The heart of any conscious, abundant business is *people,* and nothing can happen when you have zero connection with other humans.

Take a moment to think about this. All resources, including time, energy, and money, can be circulated when you are connected to people. GUS loves to deliver messages and wild synchronicities through interactions and connections with people. It's amazing how much of our energy fields open to receiving abundance when we are willing to be seen deeply through real relationships and connections with others, including our teams, our audiences, our clients, our customers, our mentors, and our business peers.

We are human beings, which means we are social beings, but we are more disconnected from each other today than at any other time in history. This can drastically slow you down on your journey to conscious success. The good news is that you don't have to spend hours each week attending networking events or speaking to scores of people to maximize the power of connection. Being present with just *one* person can open you up to the energy of the entire grid of humanity, and a single aligned connection is all it takes to open the door to an entire network of opportunities and partnerships that can accelerate business growth and success.

So, even when you're deep behind the scenes in your business and do not feel like talking or reaching out to anyone, take a moment to do just one thing that connects you to one person. It could be as simple as commenting on a social media post or making an old-school phone call to another entrepreneur in your area. It really doesn't matter what you do because your intention and the action you take to reach out to someone is enough to activate the power of connection, which can lead to unexpected friendships, mutually beneficial relationships with business partners and peers, and incredibly lucrative projects that can eventually get you to your business goals.

The Power of Curiosity

The *power of curiosity* holds the energy of inquiry and movement and expansion. It keeps everything fresh, energized, and alive. Any time you conclude that something's going to happen in a specific way, you're limiting the energy that flows to it—and you're restricting the expansion of it.

A lot of entrepreneurs love mapping out their business, lasering in on a goal, and getting specific about how good life's going to be when they get there. It's fun to think that if we just take it step-by-step, everything will go exactly as we plan, but the reality is very different. The minute we draw a conclusion around a plan or draw a conclusion around how things are going to go, we officially shut ourselves off from the path of least resistance that allows us to uncover the fastest, the most exciting, and the most fun path. That's the path that's most in alignment with our own purpose and calling.

This doesn't mean that you don't get to choose your path or choose an option, but it's about choosing and then still staying open to all the possibilities *other* than what you chose. This is not about getting particularly excited or attached to a specific choice, decision, or opportunity that's popping up; it's about getting excited about the fact that GUS is working for your highest good. It's about getting excited that things are moving and getting cleared out and that different opportunities and choices are showing up for you in your business.

It's really about teaching yourself to get curious so when opportunities pop up, you're interested in what's going on, but you're not attached. When you're curious, you don't feel stuck—even when things don't go the way you hoped. Instead, you're thinking, *That didn't work out, but I'm curious to see what other opportunities might fit.*

The power of curiosity inspires and triggers movement and progression. It takes you out of ruminating and overthinking. When you're in the energy of curiosity, you stop feeling worried, doubtful, and anxious. Instead, you're thinking, *I wonder how quickly I can grow my client base and my audience on social media* or *Things are kind of chaotic right now, but I wonder how this is all going to unfold?*

When you start tapping into the excitement around that, the power of curiosity will sustain you at very high-vibrational frequencies and at a high level of consciousness so manifestations, opportunities, and synchronicities that lead you to your business goals happen in creative ways that you could not have imagined.

The Power of Creation

Here's something important you need to know about creative energy: Creation comes *through* you and not *from* you. It's about allowing yourself to become a channel for creative energy to flow.

When you tap into who you truly are and are expressing your true self, you instantly shift into a state of flow. The energy of the universe moves through you, and you are immersed in *effortless creation*. This is how we work with the power of creation to quickly move up the consciousness scale and become aligned with the frequency of the *field of infinite creation*, which is where you get to manifest in the moment.

The power of creation is about having trust, faith, and love for GUS and for yourself as you bring forth incredible, transformative ideas that can reconfigure the way things are done in business and in the world. The power of creation is pure magic because it can change everything in an instant. Creative energy is source energy; it's the energy of GUS. When it begins to flow, there's no stopping the magic that unfolds.

The key is to unlock and release all your limiting beliefs around your power to create, and one of the most effective ways to do this is to set a conscious intention to release that which no longer serves you.

True creativity happens beyond the logical mind. When we tap into the power of creation, we are moved and inspired to the core of our being—and we can easily come up with offers and create content in our businesses that's irresistible to clients and customers.

The Power of Expression

The *power of expression* is the power behind what most of us see as an "overnight success"—entrepreneurs and business owners who become industry sensations, seemingly out of nowhere. The power of expression taps into the real you, and it lets diamonds in the rough shine through as gems that can light up the world. We see this power at work all the time with videos and posts on social media that go viral. We see it with services and products that fly off the shelves. The power of expression is the magic that takes unknown names and puts them up in lights.

This power is rooted in a level of *beingness* where you are willing to follow your intuition and show up raw, real, unedited, unfiltered, and in the most potent, authentic energy available to you. It's a willingness to be seen in all your glory, and if you let it, it can change everything in your business.

However, the power of expression won't work for you if you overthink your next move or act super strategic with every little thing that you do in your business. Allow yourself to explore and experiment *in the moment* as yourself. Let yourself connect and communicate with your clients as you are and not as you think you should be.

The power of expression needs lots of room to flow and grow, and when you pay attention, you'll find that anyone who's made a significant impact or spread joy across the globe like wildfire (think J. K Rowling and the Harry Potter series) did what they were doing because they were compelled to express themselves in a field or industry that inspired them. Whether they realized it or not, they were working with the unlimited power of expression.

The Power of Spaciousness

Conscious success and abundance in business requires action, movement, and circulation, but what if you have no idea what action to take? If that's true for you, there's always one action you can take. Creating space is the default action that taps you in whenever you are confused.

Everything new needs a place to land. New ideas, new money, and new relationships all need space. Spaciousness and movement are crucial when you want to make the alignment code work for you in your business. So how do you open to fresh, vibrant, high-level energy and consciousness? Whenever you get stuck in creating space in your business, ask yourself this question: "How can I create space for something new to land and for energy to flow?"

Here are three proven techniques to kick-start your journey to tapping into the power of space:

Technique 1

Step into a genuine sense of curiosity (see the power of curiosity in this chapter). Curiosity creates space. Conclusions contract space.

Technique 2

Step into a deep meditative state. Thinking—especially overthinking and rumination—contracts space.

Technique 3

Step into a clear physical space. Clearing physical clutter, like old client files from your computer, creates physical space. This instantly translates to an energetic space that invites fresh, new high-vibrational energy, including new opportunities, contacts, and connections.

Every time you feel stuck in your business, I want you to consciously work with the power of space. It allows energy to flow so you can rapidly get back on track and begin manifesting and creating what you want in your business.

CHAPTER 11

The Awaken Code

The awaken code is about getting clear about everything that's happening in your reality. It's about being 100 percent honest with yourself about what's going on in your business and in our world. When you work with the awaken code, you'll understand—on a whole new level—that your reality is simply a reflection of your past. You'll also know how to experience the world as the version of yourself that is *already* where you want to be in future.

This might sound woo-woo or out there, but it's more grounded and more down-to-earth than you can imagine. Living in the version of yourself that is already where you want to be is about literally envisioning yourself in the future through the lens of the *biggest* vision you can come up with. When you have a vision that's so big that it scares you, it's because GUS put that vision in your heart—and you're meant to bring it into our collective reality. It's the kind of vision that opens you up and makes you start to feel the expansiveness of it. You feel deeply excited about it, but you're also nervous. It's where the pain of being outside your comfort zone and the purpose of your soul path meet. When you feel scared shitless and super excited at the same time, that's when you know you have hit the sweet spot!

It takes courage to unlock that vision and live in that vision because for most people, the ego enters the picture, which creates a massive amount of doubt. It dissolves the beautiful, empowering, everything-is-possible energy around your massive vision because you start to think, *Who am I to dream that big?* or *I can't do that yet!* or *Nope, I'm not ready for that yet!* or *That vision has nothing to do with what I'm doing,* or *That's a different path than the one I'm currently on.*

The Synchronistic Mayhem

The ego loves routine and predictability, but there's zero certainty when the path you're on is absolutely unique because it's designed *just* for you. This unique path leads directly to your soul purpose and what you're meant to do in the world, and each step is revealed in divine time. Unfortunately, this can feel like deep uncertainty to the ego even though everything is playing out exactly as it should be on an energetic level. It's essentially organized chaos or *synchronistic mayhem*.

Being in the awaken code is uncomfortable as crap! You'll find yourself pushed into acting on things that you wouldn't normally do in your business. You'll be called to take risks or try new ideas that seem crazy and make no logical sense. It's going to feel unsafe, but being guided to try new things by GUS and following those inner nudges to places that you would never go to on your own is the *safest* thing you can possibly do. The awaken code puts us into a space where our human self feels like everything's crazy and chaotic, but when you look back, you'll see that everything happened in exactly the right way at exactly the right time with exactly the right people.

I've been in the awaken code more times than I can remember. Every one of those times felt beyond crazy, confusing, and out of sync. The situations, people, challenges, timing, and obstacles that stood in my way seemed insurmountable at the time, but when I look back, it was perfectly aligned in synchronistic mayhem.

When people ask me how I became an entrepreneur, I usually say, "I don't even know!" When the awaken code is in action, it feels freaking frenetic. It feels unknown and scary. It feels like you're a quitter—and people might accuse you of being a quitter—but success is inevitable when you lean all the way into synchronistic mayhem. Everything that falls in your lap and calls you forward in the awaken code is more aligned and more abundant than anything you could've imagined or conceived on your own.

The Art of Phenomenal Growth

One of my biggest experiences with the awaken code happened when I was asked to be a business mentor for one of the top training schools for coaches. It's a school that's known worldwide for professional excellence in coaching, but when they invited me to become a mentor, I was unprepared. I had never done anything like it before, but something in me lit up at the thought of jumping in. It just *felt* right—and so I agreed.

Within a week of that first invitation—and just as I was getting comfortable with becoming a mentor—they came back to me and said, "Hey, we'd also love to get you in the classroom so you can train our coaches around the world." Training people *live* all over the world? Certifying coaches? I couldn't believe it. I couldn't even imagine it. It wasn't something I had on a vision board, and it definitely wasn't anything I was planning on doing because my business was thriving at the time.

I was seeing phenomenal growth and expansion. I was bringing in multiple five figures a month so it made absolutely no sense to go into a position with that coaching school since my thriving business would have to be put on hold! It made no sense to give up my time for income that was way below what my private clients were happy to pay me.

I've come to see that when something makes *perfect* sense to your logical, rational mind, it's not going to lead you to the edge of your potential and beyond. It's not going to take you places you couldn't have imagined, get you closer to your soul purpose, or help you rise up and serve more people. Becoming a business mentor and training coaches around the world—even though it didn't pay much at the time—put me in front of *massive* audiences and eventually led me to expanding my business *way* beyond multiple five-figures. I started serving more people at a higher level than I could have dreamed of at the time.

The awaken code asks that you learn to thrive in uncertainty and thrive in the unknown, but way too many entrepreneurs do just the opposite. They're too attached to thinking they need a crystal ball that shows them the future so they can plan out everything—down to the last detail.

Knowing how things are going to play out in advance gives people this crazy illusion of security, but it's the most unsafe place to be because if you're not leveraging your biggest gifts and following the path where you can be the biggest asset to the human race, you'll be limited, constricted, stuck, and unhappy. If you choose safety and security over following the divine path, the synchronistic mayhem, and the hell yeses that make no f'ing logical sense, you'll end up being a shadow of what you could potentially be and do in your business and in the world. I've learned this the hard way too many times when I choose logic over chaos!

So, how does synchronistic mayhem work in the awaken code? When things feel chaotic or uncertain on a human level, you need to hold on to the truth that everything's incredibly aligned on a spiritual level. Yes, it takes a deep level of trust, a deep level of knowing, a deep connection, and communication with GUS, but it's worth the effort and the courage that it takes.

The Sensible Path Is the Slowest

The logical, "sensible" path is the long, slow path. Synchronistic mayhem is chaotic, but it's the shortcut to creating what you want in your business. Most people aren't willing to fall that deeply into trust in GUS. Our egos and our minds like to let us think that it's safer *not* to do that.

We end up not making investments in our businesses, not hiring that mentor or business coach, and not going on that retreat—even though we're called to—because that would be unsafe or irresponsible. Maybe we don't do it because what we're already doing is working well.

All that logic is the mind as the saboteur. It's the ego. So, this leads back to making choices now as the highest, biggest, boldest future version of yourself. This is about skipping everything in between. The long path is thinking, *I'm seeing this current reality, and I'm going to figure out how to get to the future reality.* Guess what? You don't have to do that!

Everything you have been experiencing in your business up until this moment has simply been a reflection of the vibration that you've been putting out into the world. It's been coming back to you in a tangible form. It's been driving your decisions and actions and everything else you do.

That's the reason why so many entrepreneurs find themselves trapped on the *revenue rollercoaster ride from hell.* In that feast-or-famine cycle, their income is beyond amazing one month, but they can barely make ends meet the next month. When we're only looking at our current reality and are choosing to create based on what we're *already* experiencing, things don't go the way we want them to. We're not in the vibrational frequency or the level of consciousness we need to be to manifest and create a new reality that is different from what we know, and that's where the awaken code comes in.

Past Present and Future Present

The "present moment" isn't what most people think it is. Everything that we experience as humans is related to our pasts and to our futures, including the "now" that you're experiencing as you read this. The present moment is really a composite of two separate realities—your *past present reality* and your *future present reality.* Both these realities are constantly playing out in our consciousness—and in our energy.

Most entrepreneurs feel like they're doing the same thing again and again in their business and creating the same results because they're deep in their past present reality. Your past present reality is the container for your past present self; it's the thoughts, beliefs, fears, and doubts that were a part of your journey. It's part of what brought you to this moment. The problem is when most people look at their current reality through the lens of their past present self, they start to believe that their past holds the truth of their present—when it's really a shadow of what was and who they used to be.

This merging of the past present self and your current self—who you really are now—causes a dangerous disconnect between reality as it really is right now for you in your life and business and reality as it *used* to be for you. You end up recreating your past and making decisions that are basically something that your past present self believed and what your past present self thought about and felt and decided.

Let's pause here and reflect on the circumstances of your life right now. Reflect on your business right now. How much of what you see and what you're creating arises from your current reality *as it is*? How much of what's going on is a direct result of your current reality and is totally *disconnected* from your past?

Most entrepreneurs have a hard time trying to escape their past present reality, and their current realities are packed with obstacles, challenges, and struggles that are a result of their past beliefs and decisions. When you invest your time and energy, you get totally caught up in fixing every single one of those problems.

A Metaconscious Truth Alert

I want you to hold this metaconscious truth alert in your heart and mind for the rest of your time here on earth: we can't have a fresh start, we can't shake off the mistakes and missteps of our past, and we can't create something that has never been created before—a new product, service, innovation, a new way of doing business, a new way of seeing the world and experiencing the world—if we're *merged* with our past present reality.

Albert Einstein said, "We cannot solve our problems with the same thinking we used when we created them," but this is where we pour so much of our energy. It pulls us away from the field of infinite creation and our future present reality, which is a living space that is continuously being created, moment by moment, in our current reality. Our future present reality is the place where anything and everything is possible; all possibilities exist there, and none of it is accessible or attainable when we're stuck in the past.

So, how do you disconnect from your past present reality? How do you break free so you can stop creating your current reality *from* your past present reality? I want you to do some sleuthing. Put on your investigator's cap and go looking for stories. Keep your eye out for stories you tell yourself, beliefs that you've held for a long time, and thought patterns and behaviors that keep playing out on an endlessly repeating loop. These are signs that you are merged with your past present reality.

For instance, if your income stream isn't what you want it to be in your business, take some time out to journal or reflect on the stories and patterns that are living in your heart, mind, and consciousness. Think about what you believe around money and wealth—the ideas and thoughts that continue to create and recreate your past. Check if your past present reality is showing up in your bank account and in your ability to create wealth, keep wealth, and make money. Whatever it may be, check if that reality keeps showing up in your business, your ability to attract dream clients, and opportunities that keep eluding you.

We want to uncover anything in your past present reality that is coming from a place of lack. A massive clue that your past present reality is running the show operating from a sense of "not enoughness." If you see not enough opportunities, not enough clients, not enough money, not enough time, not enough, not enough, not enough, it keeps you recreating "not enough" in your current reality.

The Antidote

So, the solution—the antidote—is to focus on creating your current reality from your future present reality. This is about tapping into that expansive, unlimited vision of everything you want to be, do, and have. This can happen when you're creating from your future present self—the version of you that already is and already has everything you're wanting to create now. It sounds complicated, but it's not. A a simple, powerful path to establishing a strong bond with your future present reality is journaling.

This is not an ordinary journaling activity where you're reflecting on the past and then trying to resolve it, shift it, change it, or make sense of it. I'm talking about journaling as a tool to step into your future present self. It's about journaling as your future present self every single morning. This is how you break the bonds of your past present self and escape your past present reality: you start on the page. Journaling as your future present self is the ultimate hack. It's a shortcut that instantly takes you into your future present reality, and it's a powerful, effective way to magnetize the bright, beautiful, effortlessly abundant energy and consciousness of your future present self into your current reality. As you align with your future present self, GUS starts arranging things. You are guided, and you receive the insights you need to create your new reality in the fastest way possible.

Intention Setting on Steroids

Journaling as your future present self is *intention setting on steroids*. I started journaling as my future present self for about five minutes every morning, but that turned into forty-five-minute sessions and then to sixty-minute sessions. I now feel like I could it all day because it's so powerful. (Don't worry. You don't have to do it for more than five minutes if you don't want to. Let your intuition guide you.) At the heart of it, this journaling exercise lets you tap into your future self, and you're basically calling that version of yourself into the now.

The most important thing is to consciously tune in to the full experience of what it's going to feel like when you manifest your biggest vision for your business. This is about getting super clear on that vision and the details of your experience, and it's about sensing and experiencing the emotion that will flow through you when everything starts to unfold the way you want it to. This usually translates to deep feelings of emotion, joy, freedom, power, beingness, and the pure, limitless essence of your true self. This is how you tap directly into the field of infinite creation and make manifestations happen in the now.

As you put pen to paper (or fingers to keyboard), I want you to imagine you already have everything you could possibly want: money in your bank account, an endless stream of ideal clients, and a beautiful conscious business that lets you give back to the world.

Connect to that vision and then ask yourself some questions:

- How would I be showing up?
- If I were booked out and on a waiting list in my business for months, how would I be showing up?
- What would I be doing?
- What would I be sharing with my audience?
- How would I be sharing what I know?
- What would I be talking about?

When you journal, you're taking your entire energetic frame of reference from where you are—and you're going straight into the future. Here are some powerful questions you can work with to kick-start your daily journaling sessions as your future present reality:

- How do I build my audience?
- What new choices would I make in my business?
- How can I play big?
- What sort of message would I share?
- If my vision already exists, and I just need to step into the next dimension to access it because it already exists, how would I be showing up?
- How can I step forward and not hold myself back?

Damn It … I Hate Paying Bills!

As you dive into this journaling activity, trust that you *will* receive the answers you're looking for. The answers will come through as long as you are living, breathing, and playing in your future present reality as your future present self instead of your past present reality as your past present self.

So, when we start to take action and step into future present reality, we can sometimes feel ourselves reverting back to looking at our past present reality or even our current reality and treating it as our *only* reality—and that's when we end up recycling our problems and recreating the past.

When I stepped into my future present self, I created the $100,000 that I talked about in chapter 10. A few weeks later I doubled that to $200,000 in ninety days. I was journaling as my future present self every single day. Every single morning, I consciously stepped into my future present self, and my entire current reality started to transform around me. I started to see everything as my future present self, and I was showing up as my future present self. I was coaching and teaching as my future present self, and I was making every single decision in my business as my future present self. You don't have to "become better," "change your habits," "overcome blocks," or do lots of "energy practices" to live as your future present self. It's a choice. It's a decision.

When you believe you must do a lot of inner work, you'll enter this endless cycle of thinking that you need to release your beliefs or become a better person before you get to your future present reality. But that won't get you there because thinking about your blocks, issues, challenges, and beliefs that don't serve you just brings your focus back to your past present reality. It gets you thinking as your past present self and recreating more of your past, and that's how we end up in a spin and in an ongoing loop that could last months, years, or decades—and maybe forever. When you understand how your past present reality works, you'll see that it is simply a reflection of your thoughts, emotions, and energetic being-ness from the past, and it's about stepping into the energetic beingness as your future present self.

For instance, let's imagine you're paying the bills in your business and you think, *Damn it ... I hate paying bills!* You're totally stressed. This is you being in your past present reality. This is you paying your bills as your past present self. What you want to do is shift into the emotional space where you can feel money flooding into your business, and it's like tens of thousands of dollars just flooding into your bank account. This is your future present reality, and when you get into that space and pay your bills from that space, you're paying your bills from your future present self.

I started to make choices as my future present self long before my future reality became my current reality. I invested close to a hundred thousand dollars in my business pretty much at the start of my business because I made decisions from my future present self. If I am so deep in my knowing that I am running a seven-figure or multiple-seven-figure empire, I'm not going to pinch pennies on investing in my business!

Stepping into Future Present Reality

A friend I met online became very upset when she was not accepted into an application-based online program that I had created. It was not because she wasn't good enough or anything like that; it was because she was just starting out, and the level of support in that program would not have been beneficial to her. So, when she was upset about not being accepted and told me how she felt, my past present self with all my old hang-ups and beliefs kicked in big-time.

When I was a kid, I would always take responsibility for other people's feelings. I believed I was responsible for how people felt. It was something that was given to me very early on as a child—that I was responsible to make other people happy. I believed it was my job to make sure that people didn't get upset, that I didn't disappoint them, that I didn't let them down, that I didn't hurt their feelings, that I didn't reject them, and that everybody was always feeling good around me.

So, all that past stuff came up when I found out that this friend was not happy with what went down. When I stepped into my future present reality, I asked, "How would my future present self handle this?" I realized instantly that I would have boundaries in place that would make me inaccessible to people projecting their fears and sense of lack onto me. This awareness allowed me to embrace setting these boundaries on a mental and emotional level, and that was enough to change the game. I could let go of that need to please and the need to take on other people's feelings as my responsibility.

Sometimes, you can't really implement what your future present self would do. For instance, if you have a lot of administrative tasks on your plate, and your future present self would have their personal assistant get that done, you might not be in the place where hiring a full-time assistant makes financial sense. Instead, you can start to move in the *energy* of that direction. You could start asking around for referrals, checking out pricing, or listing the administrative tasks that you'd hand off to your VA when you eventually hire someone. This is a very effective way to step into your future present self—and step into the beingness of it—even while you're completing those annoying administrative tasks in your business in your current reality.

We can't change our existing, current reality until we step into our future present reality. When you are in alignment with the energy of your future present self, everything else arranges itself to create your future present reality in your current reality. All you need to do is show up and let GUS show you how to share your message and make choices in your business that are perfectly relevant for where you are and what you want to create.

PART III

THE TRUTH ABOUT ACCELERATED GROWTH IN A CONSCIOUS BUSINESS

CHAPTER 12

Conscious Business Rule 1: Start a Movement and Not a Following

Above all things, our deepest desire in business (and life) is to *belong*. It's not to make more money, write a bestseller, be famous, have a million followers, or any of the other external "success milestones" we find ourselves chasing. Long before we got to the place where getting "more, more, more" became the central, burning goal, we all wanted to simply *belong*. We are born with this desire because belonging is about being a part of something greater, something that matters. It's about connecting. It's about finding *our* people. It's about aligning our hearts and souls and moving our vision forward *together*.

So many old-school business principles and concepts are about growing a massive audience of followers and fans and then getting to a higher place, to stand "above," and then do whatever it takes to reinforce that position and be recognized as the number one guru, expert, or authority. It's about being validated and recognized.

You don't have to give up on any of those goals, but it's important to go deep and reflect on *why* you want what you want. When you want to achieve greatness, prosperity, and fame in your business because you secretly long to be loved, adored and followed by others, when your desire to become the most successful person you know is because you want to be better than everyone else, when that's the driving force behind everything you do in your business, it's an unmistakable sign that the energy collapsers—attachment, judgment, and fear (see chapter 8)—are running your life.

Stacy Hartmann

Sure, building a following can accomplish a lot of external goals and provide happiness, but sooner or later, you'll end up feeling like something is missing—no matter how much wealth and abundance you accumulate, no matter how many incredible goals you achieve, and no matter how many prizes, rewards and awards you happen to get.

People say, "It's lonely at the top," but what if there isn't a "top" to get to? What if this isn't just about being an expert or a leader? What if it's not about being the best? This doesn't mean leadership ceases to exist or that you don't have to hit your highest potential. It just means that change-makers, trailblazers, visionaries, and leaders in business who want to create real change in the world and a new, empowering way of doing business that is inclusive, loving, generous, and massively profitable need to come from a space of love, community, and equality. This new empowering, abundant business landscape can happen—and it will happen—when we lead from the intention of finding the greater good for all and not just for individual fulfillment.

Conscious business rule 1 states, "I'm on the front lines; let's pave this path to joy, wealth, and fulfillment together." When your audience, your followers, your fans, and your clients and customers start to see that they are *just* as powerful and limitless as you are—the business leader, the expert, the coach, or the author—they will stop putting you on a pedestal and start locking arms with you and each other to build an incredibly transformational alliance of energy. That is the kind of energy that creates and recreates worlds. So, if you have a burning desire, ambition, or purpose—an *obsession*—to make a *real* difference in the world, focus on starting a movement and not a following.

CHAPTER 13

Conscious Business Rule 2: Don't Be Someone Else's Clone. Do Your Own Thing

If you've been on Facebook, Instagram, or any other social platform for more than a few minutes, you've probably noticed a bunch of ads crossing your newsfeed. I've seen hundreds and hundreds of ads, and just about every ad starts to look like the others with a different name slapped on top. It's so boring!

A few years ago, there was a trend where just about every online female entrepreneur had a professional, branded photo series shot at the beach. She was sitting with her computer and some sort of drink in her hand. She was smiling in the sunshine. She was diving into the ocean or gazing at a gorgeous sunset. The photos were supposed to depict a picture-perfect laptop life. It was what success was supposed to look like, especially for online business owners—and there were other trends too.

There were ads where entrepreneurs dyed their hair bright pink or purple or green or had huge tattoos on their necks or arms. These ads were about business coaching or strategy or some other service or product. Just to be clear here—it's all good if pink hair and neck tattoos are really who you are, but those images made me stop. They made me wonder if these people were showing up as themselves. Was any of it a true reflection of their unique essence? Intuitively, it felt like most of them were just doing something—anything—to look different so they'd stand out. They had it all wrong.

The truth is there's no need to "do anything" to stand out because there's only one real way to be truly unique. It's a rare and real thing that instantly grabs attention and creates an irresistible vortex of attraction: Be you. Be brave enough to be who *you* truly are because you're already unique. You're already special. There's only one of you in the whole world. Show up as yourself and share the full expression of who you are. This is about sharing your unique essence across all aspects of your business: in your writing, in your videos, and in how you show up for your clients. It's the thing that gets people to start thinking, *Who the heck is she? I have to know more!*

Being yourself is simple, but it's not easy. So many entrepreneurs have no idea what their unique essence is. It's about diving deep into the energy of expression that radiates from you even when you don't say a word. You can identify this energy by asking yourself a few questions. For instance, are you naturally mysterious? Maybe you have a light, fun element to your energy? You might be deep, introspective, or even dark? Are you airy? Humorous? Slow and thoughtful? Maybe you're fast and energetic?

Way too many entrepreneurs look at what's already being done by successful leaders and businesses so they can show up in the exact same way. They think following someone else's footsteps will get them to their goals. This never works because searching for answers outside your own powerful, intuitive essence instantly creates a disconnect between your inner wisdom and the distinctive, exceptional creative treasures of your own soul—the gifts that only you have to give. You end up losing pretty much all the magic of your essence, and you become a weak reflection of someone else.

Your soul has its own language, and that energy can turn into new words—*your* words—that have the power to magnetize your ideal clients and customers. What does your soul really want to express? What do you want to say that you're terrified you'll be burned at the stake for saying or even thinking? So many entrepreneurs stifle, suppress, and repress their energy of expression, and instead of presenting themselves as who they are, they dilute their personalities so they'll be liked and accepted.

When you show up potent in your thoughts, feelings, and being, you're like a stiff drink. With just one sip, your audience is "love drunk," and even more than that, they get the sense that you were meant to cross paths with you. They believe it's their destiny to be in your energy, to grow and learn from you, and to work with you.

It happens when you step up and decide to be yourself—the revolutionary, one-of-a-kind leader you are—instead of doing and being what you *think* people are looking for. Instead of being obsessed with your reputation and how people *perceive* you—or being consumed by fear of rejection—you unapologetically step deeper into you and express yourself as no one else but you.

There's only one regret I want to avoid at the end of each day in my business, and it's that I didn't show up in my fullest expression. If I fully honor my identity, who I am in my heart and soul and at my core, then I know my job is done. Remember, like energy attracts like energy (see chapter 1, principle 5). So, if you want to truly manifest your biggest opportunities, business partners, clients, and customers, the "mask of likeability" has to come off. You need to do *you*.

When you show up fully as yourself and in your energetic potency, you'll open yourself up to the magic of consciousness and energy, and you'll quickly have everything you desire. Show up how you think you are supposed to show up—or in a way you think people want to see you—and you'll attract the lower levels of consciousness that reinforce and perpetuate the unwanted reality you are striving to change. We can't blaze our own trails if we're trying to follow somebody else's path. Defy normal or become invisible—you get to decide.

CHAPTER 14

Conscious Business Rule 3: Slow Down to Speed Up

Best-selling author and founder of the phenomenal coaching school, iPEC, Bruce Schneider says, "Doing is work. Being is effortless." I couldn't agree more! This doesn't mean you don't take action. It's *not* about sitting around and waiting for things to work out for you or fall into your lap. It just means that most people who do a lot and invest a ton of time and energy into achieving their goals are getting what they want through pure effort and focused concentration from their minds. There's a better way, a faster way, and a more easeful way: show up as you are and then listen for clues and signs for your next steps. This is the secret formula that collapses time.

The mind can only create the longest path available because what we're doing is collecting, consolidating, and making sense of information from *all* of our past experiences, beliefs, and perceptions. We have millions of "mental files" carefully stored away in our conscious and unconscious, and as a result, the thinking mind has access to a massive amount of information and knowledge. It adds a bunch of details and complexity to everything we try to do—we really are too smart for our own good—and then we motivate ourselves and fill ourselves up with tenacity, grit, and a kind of crazed drive to get to what we want at *any* cost.

This is the entrepreneur's addiction to doing, doing, and more doing, and I see it all the time. We're all hustling, pushing, striving, falling off track, getting back on track, doing everything right, following the "rules and guidelines," and we never stop.

Metaconscious Entrepreneur

Then we realize that our goals are a moving target. Every time we manage to arrive at one goal, there's a new one to reach, a new target to hit, another long path ahead of us.

We keep looking for the next level, and there's always going to be a next level waiting for us. There is always more to do, more to accomplish, and more to achieve. There's always another problem to solve, another email to respond to, or another fire to put out. Before we know it, months, years, and maybe even decades go by. We feel like we'll never "get there," and the sad truth is that many entrepreneurs spend their entire lives looking ahead, never stopping long enough to fully experience the beauty, abundance, joy, and love that's right here, right now.

At the start of my business, all I wanted was to use my gifts as a coach, have more freedom, and replace my annual nine-to-five income, which was $60,000 a year at the time. Well, I accomplished all of that in the first six months in my business! But guess what? I wasn't happy! My human conditioning didn't allow me to feel the happiness and fulfillment that I thought I'd feel. Instead, I came up with a new goal almost instantly. This time, I wanted to create a six-figure business in six months. When I hit that too, I immediately moved on to multiple six figures and then seven figures. I had to have more, more, more. One day, I finally stopped long enough to ask myself a question: "Why do I want to hit these goals?" The answer came through: "Because once you get to those goals, you'll have *freedom*—money and time freedom—to do whatever you want, whenever you want!"

My ego shouted, "Yes! Exactly!" However, something in my soul called out to me to go deeper, and when I continued to reflect, another question popped into my heart and mind:

"How much freedom do you have right here and now?" The honest answer was that I *already* had everything I was striving so hard for. The worst part? I was sacrificing everything I already had because I believed it could only come from accomplishing the next goal and the next. In other words, I was giving up all my freedom pursuing more freedom! I was so busy *doing*, there was very little *being*:

- being in the beauty of life
- being in the freedom
- being in the love
- being in the connection
- being in the peace
- being in the fun
- being in the joy
- being in the laughter

When did everything get so dang serious? I realized it was time to lighten up. In fact, I even went so far in this realization that I was already whole and complete that I did a full 180 and let everything *go*. I was tired and burned out, and even though my business was successful, my soul was dying. It was suffocating with all the doing and being strangled in the pursuit of more. When I let everything go, my soul's whispers started to become louder, and magical things started to happen. The more I listened to what my soul was asking me to do—instead of following the path my mind told me to take—the more I got to experience flow, ease, peace, and abundance.

So just *being*, and slowing down, was actually collapsing time and speeding everything up. I was creating more wealth and having more synchronistic opportunities fall in my lap, gracefully and effortlessly. I was being pulled forward by a powerful force; on the outside, it still looked like I was busy, but on the inside, *everything* was different. My actions were overflowing with anticipation, excitement, and curiosity. It felt like time stood still—and superhuman productivity kicked in. Before, my actions felt forced, and it felt like despite working on my business for ten hours a day, I was barely getting anything done.

Now, I was creating entire courses and all the marketing funnels around them and having everything up and running in less than a week—something that would ordinarily take months to create—because I was no longer taking action from my mind. I was getting out of my own way and allowing higher wisdom to come through. When I slowed down, I could hear my intuition, inner whispers, and guidance from GUS, and I did not take *any* action unless it came from my soul.

Slowing down to speed up is about creating space instead of doing, doing, doing. When all we do is take action, the energetic vibration slows way down because the energy has nowhere to go and nowhere to flow. Energy needs space for superhuman productivity, wild abundance, and success to happen. Energy needs space to make magic. When we are present—just *being* and relishing in the highest vibrational emotions and the highest levels of consciousness—everything speeds up because we're creating space. That's what collapses time, and it is magic!

CHAPTER 15

Conscious Business Rule 4: The More Chaotic Things Feel in the Human Realm, the More Organized They Are in the Spiritual Realm

The only real way to transform your reality and your business is to move beyond the mind. We can create a new reality when we learn to tap into the database of consciousness—the quantum field—where all things exist, including the things that we have *never* experienced. So, if you're stuck recreating the same results in your business, day after day, month after month, year after year, it means you're relying solely on your mind—and you're ignoring your intuition and the signs and messages from GUS to accomplish your desires.

There are two key elements that get in our way when we come up with business ideas and strategies purely from the space of the mind. First, our minds are limited to seeing everything through the lens of the past (see chapter 11, "The Awaken Code"). This means our minds draw conclusions and create from our past experiences; anything the mind conceives is simply a recreation of what *was*. Second, the mind is amazing at organizing information so it "makes sense," and because the mind is limited, the more things "make sense," the more you are limiting your true power.

When everything's 100 percent predictable and sequential, it simply means we're controlling our dreams with our limited mind power and not opening to all possibilities that exist beyond anything our minds could conceive. As you already know, the field of infinite creation is where limitless possibility exists, and this often feels chaotic and illogical to the limited human mind.

We talked about the magic of divine orchestration, synchronistic grid, and the power of the field of infinite creation in the fifth precept: Effort is limited, energy is limitless (see chapter 5), and the synchronistic grid is divine organization. Imagine GUS as a being who is above the entire earth, above all the galaxies, above everything that exists, and beyond infinite space. Talk about the *ultimate* bird's-eye view and from this space—GUS sees *all* things and knows all things.

GUS is where magical insights come from, and that's why the insights and guidance we receive make zero sense to our logical minds. The less sense it makes, the more powerful it is—and the more it collapses time.

It feels chaotic because it's divinely organized, which is what we call *synchronicity*. That is why messages, ideas, downloads, insights, intuition, and whatever else we receive from GUS seem to come through to us out of nowhere. So, when we do receive these insights, our job is to take the action on this material realm as quickly as humanly possible.

Remember the ice-cream shop story (see chapter 8, "Understanding the Seven Levels of Consciousness")? Well, what happened after that was *pure* magnificence and synchronicity. It was probably the most vulnerable experience I've had in my life. It was mind-blowing. (I think that's where the phrase "mind blowing" comes from because we finally get out of our heads!). At the time of that incident, I had just lost my grandma. I can feel myself getting emotional about it even now.

She had a massive heart attack on Thanksgiving Day with the whole family there. We had a *very* close relationship, and my grandma was this cool, funky, old lady. She believed in biorhythms, she would play bingo based on her horoscope, and she was all about numerology. She was totally not like the norm, especially for someone in her age group. She was so tapped in, and I had a really special relationship with her because I also knew that I had some really interesting spiritual gifts—ever since I was a little girl. After she passed, I was going through a phase when I had all these challenges in my career. I started to feel a really strong presence supporting me and guiding me, and I knew it was Grandma.

The ice-cream shop that I visited that day used to be my grandma's restaurant, which is located in a town near where I live. So, the day I went there, it was because I had this massive urge to go. I didn't know *why* I wanted to go; I just knew I had to go even though life was beyond busy back then. I had small kids running around and a lot going on at work, so I kept putting it off.

One night, my husband and I got into this massive fight (looking back, it feels like I created the drama as an excuse to go to the damn ice-cream shop!). In the middle of that fight, I felt like I needed to get out of the house, and off I went to the ice-cream shop.

As soon as I walked in, the owner started talking to me. He was a jovial, kind man, and he asked what I wanted to do. I told him about my work with young people (I was a juvenile probation officer at the time) and the impact I was longing to have on these kids. I talked about how I wanted to find a way to create more sustainable funding to support this program that would be so helpful for so many kids, and as you know, the rest is history!

We ended up creating this amazing business partnership that transformed countless young lives. So, the more things make sense and the more logical they are, the more likely they are actually coming from the limited mind. The more chaotic things seem, the more they are coming from the spiritual realm, which is where amazing, incredible abundance flows.

CHAPTER 16

Conscious Business Rule 5: Quitting Is Starting

In my last real-world, nine-to-five job as a probation officer, we created a program that had a success rate above 90 percent in significantly reducing dropout rates among disadvantaged youth. We raised $250,000 in two years to deliver the program, and almost every funder we approached said yes without missing a beat There were truly no challenges with it.

The whole thing went on to become an incredible success. We watched as students who were failing made it to honor roll in just one semester. Kids who couldn't get onto their sports teams at school or qualify for any kind of sports event were being recruited by college teams. Some kids became the first person in their families to be accepted into college. It was—without a shadow of a doubt—a wildly successful and impactful program for hundreds of disadvantaged youths who otherwise would have fallen through the cracks.

The idea for this program and the unlimited creative energy that I received came directly from GUS because I was open to receiving it. This energy cleared all blocks, obstacles, and challenges. We faced no challenges in putting together that complex operation.

Then, something unthinkable happened. At the height of all this unprecedented success, I was guided to stop working with disadvantaged youths altogether. I was guided to leave my job as a probation officer, and it made no sense at the time. I had no idea where I was going to go next, but I knew I had to go.

Stacy Hartmann

I already knew enough about GUS and the field of infinite creation to understand that I had to take this nudge—this urge to leave—seriously, and I did. I walked away, and as expected, it upset a lot of people in my community and in my hometown. Many board members of the organizations I was partnering with called me a "quitter." I'm not going to lie; it hurt. A lot. I remember talking to a good friend about how much it pained me to leave even though I knew I was doing the right thing. I felt like I was abandoning people and letting them down. I felt like I was depriving hundreds of youths the opportunity to thrive, and my heart ached at the thought.

And then she said something that instantly made sense and brought so much relief. She said, "You're not a quitter; you're a starter." As soon as she said that, it felt like an elephant had been lifted off my chest. In that instant, I tuned in to the truth that I somehow already knew in my bones: my gifts and contributions to humanity were being called forward in a much bigger way. I had no clue what that really meant, but I trusted GUS. I knew in my heart, in my mind, and in my soul that I was doing exactly what I was supposed to do to fulfill a much greater purpose.

This trust, this knowing, gave me an invisible bulletproof jacket around people who couldn't understand why I was making the choices I was making. I knew how it looked to the outside world. I knew that it didn't make sense that I was leaving a job that I was good at, something that allowed me to help countless young people. I knew it didn't make sense and that it wasn't logical, but I also knew that when GUS says go, I need to go—and when GUS says stay, I need stay.

I listen.

The key thing for you, me, and everyone else is to get quiet and listen every single day. Tune in to those subtle feelings, those emotions, that intuition that tells you exactly what to do. That's GUS speaking to you, and you need to listen to those ideas, insights, and input and then take action fast—even if it's scary. And it's scary about 90 percent of the time!

Experiences like this have taught me that when we are truly listening to GUS, it often means being able to pivot and turn on a dime. Life can start to feel like a series of disconnected events. The dots don't always fully connect until you look back when it's all over. Then it makes sense—divine, aligned, perfect sense. I'm no longer worried about quitting or being logical or consistent. I go where GUS guides me to go. I do what GUS guides me to do.

I've found that the only thing we need to be fully consistent with is listening and acting on GUS's guidance, and the only thing we need to be obsessed about is our purpose, our path, and our truth. In order do what we are meant to do, sometimes we must quit what we're already doing. Even when things are *good*, letting them go for something *great* and then letting that go for something *transcendental* is what we do as metaconscious entrepreneurs. When you begin cultivating a deep trust in GUS, you get to start on the path to greatness. You get to access drop-you-to-your-knees possibilities. You get to achieve dreams that are bigger, brighter, and bolder than you could have dreamed for yourself because GUS's dream for you is always more than you can possibly imagine. It's all there—it's all within your reach—but only if you're ready to quit.

CHAPTER 17

Conscious Business Rule 6: The Customer Is Not Always Right

Anyone who encounters your business will have a unique experience because they're looking at what's going on and experiencing what's happening through their own unique lenses. People see the world based upon their own unique programming and past conditioning. They're looking at the world through the filters of their *beliefs,* their *identities,* their *challenges,* their *life experiences,* and on and on.

So, when you get input and feedback from your clients and customers, you need to take a minute to think about what's really going on. Feedback—whether it's positive or negative—is your opportunity to grow in your awareness and to be honest and check in with your intentions behind the actions and decisions you make in your business. It's also incredibly important to be discerning and to honestly evaluate what people are saying.

I'm talking about *radical responsibility,* which means cultivating the skills to recognize when you're acting out of alignment with your values. This is about knowing when your choices are coming from ego, when you're putting your own business and profits ahead of your customer's needs, or when you are out of integrity with GUS.

If you learn that your intentions are in full alignment with your values, and you know you're consistently taking action from higher levels of consciousness—level 5 and above—you can get a good night's sleep knowing that everything you do is ultimately for your customers' highest good, no matter what kind of feedback you get.

Keep in mind that everything you experience, think, feel, and believe is your response to *your* current level of consciousness, and everything someone else experiences, thinks, feels, and believes is simply their response to *their* current level of consciousness. As Austrian neurologist psychiatrist, Holocaust survivor, and author of the transformational, classic *Man's Search for Meaning*, Viktor Frankl said, "Between stimulus and response there is a space. In that space is our power to choose our response. In our response lies our growth and our freedom."

That space between stimulus and response is where *all* our power lies. Most people respond by default based on their past programming and conditioning, and they end up recreating their past (no surprise there!). It's important to know that the gap between stimulus and response is so small it's almost imperceptible, but if we widen that gap and create space in between, we make room for some magic to come through. It is in that space where we have the power to choose our responses, and this is the birthright of every living soul on the planet.

When it comes to customer feedback, we want to stay in that gap—and we want to widen that gap so we can clearly see what's actually going on versus what we think is going on. But we simply can't do this if we follow the "rule" that the customer is always right. If we end up taking on responsibility for others, we end up getting lost in criticism, faultfinding, complaining, and victimhood.

By making the customer right and taking responsibility for something that is theirs, we can actually limit them, which keeps them from reaching their full power and potential. We can do unforeseen harm that perpetuates a self-fulfilling travesty that will play out over and over again. So, instead of making the customer right—and you wrong—take the time to play, experiment, and reflect inside the gap between stimulus and response.

These key questions can give you insight and clarity about what's really going on:

- Are my choices and decisions in alignment with my values?
- Am I coming from ego?
- Am I truly acting, thinking, and doing in a way I can be proud of?
- Are my intentions pure and in service of the highest good of all?

If your answers are yes, know that any reaction the customer has is 100 percent theirs and has nothing whatsoever to do with you.

CHAPTER 18

Conscious Business Rule 7: You Were Born to Create and Not Just Consume

Like it or not, we live in a hustle-worshipping world that is geared toward a "I need more" and "I'm not enough" culture. Nothing is ever enough, and we feel we need to invest more time, more money, and more energy all the time. We're encouraged to totally ignore what we truly think and feel, and we're constantly looking at others who have achieved "massive success" so we can get there too. There is a *huge* cost to this—a massive downside. When we look to others to guide us toward fulfillment and joy in our lives—when we crave material success, praise, and recognition—we are repressing our creative powers.

Success, as the world defines it, is limited to what already exists. It's what someone already believed, thought about, innovated, created, or manifested. So, when we adopt the world's definition of success, we're reinventing what already *is*. The truth is what already exists has brought us to where we are today, but it will not be the thing that takes us up to the higher levels of consciousness evolution and personal growth.

While it's important to focus on creation over consumption, it's not "wrong" to consume. You're reading this book—consuming it—and many before it because you *love* to learn. However, you need to have clear awareness of *why* you are learning. If you are consuming information to learn and create from that learning, it's all good. That's *clean consumption*. If you're consuming from an energetic space of "not enoughness" and trying to "correct" an aspect of yourself you are judging as wrong or imperfect, you will embody that exact belief and see everything you learn through that lens. That means you'll reinforce it, rather than shift it, and that's *dirty consumption.*

You can tune in to clean consumption versus dirty consumption based on the three powerful intentions that fuel all consumption:

1. Consumption for Inspiration

    When we read or absorb information from someone who has written or is expressing from their quantum powers of expression and creation, we entrain to that energy. We align to the energy where the content was created and feel our own expression and creativity coming alive. This is clean consumption because it's a conduit to the higher self and to the database of consciousness or field of infinite creation. This is where we are consuming for the purpose of entrainment instead of information. As soon as the spark happens and we are tapped in, the content has passed the baton from the other person's genius to yours, and this naturally leads to the moment when we stop consuming and start creating.

2. Consumption for the Pure Joy of It

    As metaconscious entrepreneurs who want to create and serve at the highest levels of consciousness, we need to understand that feeling a sense of joyous creative flow is not a luxury; it is an absolute necessity. When we become lost in a book or a story or lose track of time as we write content for our businesses, we are in the energy of joyous, creative flow. This happens when we are reading, learning, and consuming solely for the high-vibrational frequencies we are experiencing in the moment. This is clean consumption because we experience ease and a sense of lightness, and it validates the intention for the consumption in the first place, which was to simply to feel good and experience joyous, creative flow.

3. Consumption for Learning

This type of consumption can be a little bit tricky because it can be clean or dirty depending on how you work with it. Consuming or learning so you can gain better skills has to do with the human aspect of being. If I share my expression via video, I may want to learn how to use the software. This is information that can't be gleaned from the database of collective consciousness. However, others have done these tactical things before, and I can learn from them.

The key is only consuming for skill set mastery for the step that is directly in front of you. I encourage you to work with the *one-by-four model*: for every hour of learning, you want to spend four hours implementing or creating and then connecting back into source for the next insight to act upon. Once the next insight comes in, take the action until you hit a point where another tactical skill will be helpful. This is clean consumption.

If you are learning because you're putting off the next action step, that's dirty consumption. We all know entrepreneurs who purchase the latest course, training, book, retreat, program, and so on because they want to "learn more." In reality, they're not doing the thing they need to do, which is taking action.

So, learn the skill and put it into action. Focus on the one step right in front of you and don't get wrapped up in the rest of the steps. It takes trust and knowing that you will figure it out every step of the way. You don't have to see the whole path to keep moving. This honors the flow, and it allows the exponential time-saving, energy-saving, and abundance-creating shortcuts that only clean consumption that leads to creation can provide.

CHAPTER 19

Creating Unstoppable Synergy, Growth, and Abundance for the Highest Good of All

Imagine you're checking your bank account. You see how much money you have in there, and it's *not* looking good. If you believe what you see is your *only* reality, you might think, *I don't have enough in here. How am I gonna make it work this month?* This is a low-consciousness response because you're experiencing uncomfortable emotions. There is probably some fear and anxiety—and maybe even some guilt or shame. You're *reacting* with your energy based on what you see with your physical eyes, and it translates into disruptive, negative emotions. It feels like suffering, it feels like upset, it feels like pain, and it feels like other low-energy emotions. This energy perpetuates your unwanted "not enough money" situation. What you focus on with your energy expands, and "not enough money" keeps happening in your reality.

Whenever we feel like victims or feel powerless about situations, events, and circumstances, we end up recreating the same experiences over and over again. It becomes an endless cycle because we are obsessed with what we *see,* believing it's our only reality. A deep, absolutely limitless wellspring of energy is flowing through us.

You are already connected to the ultimate source of energy—GUS and the quantum field or the field of infinite creation—and that is where all possibilities exist. The most effective way to tap into this energy and allow it to flow through you so you can create, invent, innovate, and shape how you want to run your business and live is to embrace the *shadow side*—the parts of you that are negative, painful, or even hateful—and not just the aspects that are loving, patient, or kind.

The Pathway

When we focus on what we see, hear, touch, and hold, our energy is diminished—and everything stops working. You've probably experienced this in your business. Maybe you've tried following all the "right" strategies. You're doing all the things. You're showing up and sharing value with your audience on social media every day. You're building funnels, writing emails, and creating blog posts. You're networking and connecting with ideal customers, but nothing much happens because you have a *diminished energetic field*—and people don't feel drawn to responding to you.

Metaconscious entrepreneurs consistently, consciously, and intentionally work with energy, and when we do, everything starts to flow. You could show up the same way or write the exact same post on social media, but this time, but using conscious intentionality, going deep, and being you, it *will* be different. This time, it's infused with your true energy. This time, it's infused with your power. This time, it's infused with your light and magnetism. This time, it calls in all the right people and the right results for your business.

This is where you step out of victimhood and start to see that nothing has any power or control over you and what you create. The second you come into that wholeness and that completeness and the realization that "I am the creator of my reality, I am 100 percent in power, and I control everything that is happening in my world with my energy," you start to align with wealth and anything and everything that you desire. That's how you create unstoppable synergy, growth, and abundance. It begins with embracing all of who you are, including your shadow side. That's the pathway to coming into full power and hitting the highest levels of consciousness (levels 5, 6, and 7).

Embracing All of You

The concept of the shadow originates from the psychology of Carl Jung. The shadow comprises the aspects of you that you don't like and don't want to acknowledge. It's easy for us to feel happy and accept ourselves when we feel happy with ourselves. When we feel good about ourselves, we feel uplifted, energized, excited, inspired, and creative. We feel all the feelings and emotions that are on the higher levels of consciousness.

We think that we just need to be "good" to rise to a higher consciousness, but this doesn't work in the long run because we're ignoring what we believe to be "bad." Jealousy, craving, addiction, pain, disgust, and contempt are the darker aspects of human nature. We want so much to reject all of that, but we need to accept all of it because it's only at the deepest level of acceptance—when we accept ourselves in the aspects that we have judged as repelling—that we can truly rise into higher consciousness.

A lot of spiritual and personal growth methods leave our shadows ... in the shadows! Most people are way too busy trying to get up to the light. They're clamoring and clamoring and clamoring, and they get exhausted because they think that the light is "up there." I invite you to dig deep into the darkest aspects of your psyche, which is where your shadows live. True spiritual freedom, limitless creativity, and consciousness at the highest levels come from going down into the shadows and not just up into the light.

When we go deep into the shadows, something happens. Our false beliefs, our false personas, and even the false identities and traits we want to project out to the world start to crumble and crack. What comes through is the brightest light, the most incredible, liberating freedom that you've ever experienced. When we acknowledge and accept every part of us that's been hiding in the shadows, we accelerate the *energetic alchemization process*.

Stacy Hartmann

Energetic Alchemization

Energetic alchemization is the process of accepting and embracing our light *and* our shadow, and it brings us into our full power. When we recognize that we're uncomfortable with what we're thinking and feeling, and when we're judging what's going on inside us as "negative," "wrong," or "bad," it's a chance to practice energetic alchemization. This is about becoming the witness. It's about becoming a nonjudgmental observer of what's going on inside ourselves and *accepting* that it's how we feel and it's what we think in the moment. Most of us are socialized to "be good," "think the right thing," or "feel only good feelings," and we reject ourselves. We want our thoughts and feelings to be other than what they are. And so, we end up creating separation with GUS and the field of infinite creation and diminishing our full power.

Rejection of the shadow keeps our energy fragmented as opposed to coming into whole power. When we're in whole power, we are one with GUS—and we are one with the field of infinite creation, which is where manifestations and creations happen just like *that*.

Conscious Wealth versus Shadow Wealth

Money is an incredible vehicle that we get to use when we can create wealth and circulate it out in the world from a place of wholeness and completeness. When you consciously create wealth to live an incredible human and spiritual experience, you become a role model for humanity. This is what real wealth creation looks like from a high conscious place, and ultimately, this is what it means to be a metaconscious entrepreneur.

As long as we're just trying to be "good," "perfect," or "pure" without being role models for humanity, we are not doing our part. Accepting all of who we are and showing up as ourselves is how we tip the scales in the direction of love. It's how we redefine the paradigm of wealth, and as we do that—as we consciously choose to build our businesses and circulate our money out into the world from a place of wholeness and love—we fuel the economy with love instead of greed and scarcity. This allows more and more people to get paid for their gifts.

This is conscious wealth versus shadow wealth, which is about creating wealth from a fragmented place and from rejection. Conscious wealth is not about delivering and giving wealth away so we can help other people; that would take *their* power away. I'm *not* talking about philanthropy or charity. So many "good" people think that their wealth will rescue someone, but nobody needs to be f'ing rescued! Nobody.

Everybody has their own sovereignty. Everybody has their own freedom. Everybody has the power to create their own wealth, and when we try to take our wealth and take responsibility for other people, we end up taking away their sovereign power and their freedom. I see this all the time with female entrepreneurs. They take responsibility for their husbands. "Oh, he fucking hates his job. I want my business to take off so he doesn't have to work anymore!" That's not conscious wealth; that's shadow wealth, which is depriving people of their power.

We're metaconscious entrepreneurs; we're *not* in the business of depriving people of their power. We don't take people's power away from them. That is not what conscious wealth is for. Conscious wealth requires you to be the role model who inspires and motivates other people to find the power that is within them to create their own wealth.

Holding the Vision

So, here's what I invite you to do. Let's hold the vision for every single soul on this planet to wake up to the incredible and immense energy that is already available to them. Let's begin creating wealth from a place of energetic consciousness. Energy does not discriminate, and when we change energy, everything can change. People can stand in their power and create *miracles*; we're not doing this alone. We have GUS on our side. When we start to recognize the incredible, infinite power of energy, when we know that we can create anything, and when we help others do the same by showing them how it's done, we change business. That's how we change life. That's how we change the world.

More Resources for Growing a Wildly Successful Business that Changes the World

The Unleashed Experience

In this online course, you'll learn:

- How to build a high-vibe, high-impact business and create massive wealth with the unique activation codes you discovered in this book: the awareness code, the alignment code, and the awaken code.
- The number one question to ask yourself every single day to trigger a powerful "multiplier effect" and get to your biggest, boldest business goals (99 percent of entrepreneurs are missing the boat on this one!)
- How to harness the exclusive "Infinite Galaxy" marketing method for fast growth and mega client attraction in the shortest time possible (you will not find this *anywhere* else!)
- Exactly how to be 100 percent human and 100 percent spiritual in your being (this is the *real* key to fast, repeatable manifestations in your life and business).
- How to infuse every step in your business with future self energy for jaw-dropping magic and knock-your-socks-off success.
- The three things you *must* master to accomplish *anything* you want in your business and your life. (These are the *only* things to focus your energy on!)
- The four quantum powers that create energetic potency to instantly attract your most dreamy clients—and so much more!

To get started, visit www.UnleashedExperience.com.

The Infinite Success Accelerator

There are seven key Powers of Potential (levels of consciousness) within you, and they influence how you view everything in your business and your life. When you learn to work with these powers with clear intention, focused energy, and empowered action, there are no limits to what you can create in your business and in your life—and that's exactly what I teach you inside the Infinite Success Accelerator!

This game-changing program includes the Energy Leadership Index Assessment. This assessment is the *only* tool out there that accurately measures your current potential for success *and* gives you immediate strategies to shift into higher performance in your business based on the seven levels of consciousness discussed in this book.

It also includes four power-packed, step-by-step modules that will show you how to monetize your gifts and tap into your natural energies to create infinite success. Each module includes videos, guidebooks, and cheat sheets to help you learn and absorb the strategies and insights quickly—and have fun doing it!

To get started, visit www.InfiniteSuccessAccelerator.com.

Connect with Stacy Hartmann

I love being in touch with my readers and welcoming them to our high-vibe family. Here's how to connect with me:

1. Follow me on Facebook. This is the real me, my personal profile and not a fan page. Go to www.facebook.com/stacy.hartmann.12 and click +FOLLOW. This is where I am most active, and I frequently share thought-provoking and consciousness-raising thoughts! We'll also get to know each other more personally.
2. Sign up for my newsletter and other free resources at my website: www.StacyHartmann.com.
3. For sharing and connecting via email, reach out to me at hello@stacyhartmann.com.

www.ingramcontent.com/pod-product-compliance
Lightning Source LLC
Chambersburg PA
CBHW020432220526
45464CB00002B/665